Java Programming:
From Problem Analysis to Program Design Lab Manual

by Dr. Judy Scholl

THOMSON
™
COURSE TECHNOLOGY

D1279136

Australia • Canada • Mexico • Singapore • Spain • United Kingdom • United States

THOMSON

COURSE TECHNOLOGY

Java Programming: From Problem Analysis to Program Design Lab Manual
by Dr. Judy Scholl

Managing Editor:
Jennifer Muroff

Product Manager:
Alyssa Pratt

Development Editor:
Lisa Ruffolo, The Software Resource

Associate Product Manager:
Janet Aras

Editorial Assistant:
Christy Urban

Production Editors:
Danielle Power
Philippa Lehar

Associate Product Marketing Manager:
Angie Laughlin

Cover Designer:
Steve Deschene

Compositor:
Gex Publishing Services

Manufacturing Coordinator:
Laura Burns

Disclaimer
Course Technology reserves the right to revise this publication and make changes from time to time in its content without notice.

ISBN 0-619-15982-0

TABLE OF CONTENTS

INTRODUCTION

The objective of this lab manual is to give students step-by-step examples to become familiar with programming concepts, design, and coding. This text is designed to be used with *Java Programming: From Problem Analysis to Program Design*, but it also can be used to supplement any CS1 Java textbook. This manual is written to be used in a classroom lab environment.

FEATURES

To ensure a successful experience for instructors and students alike, this book includes the following features:

- **Lab Objectives**—Every lab has a brief description and list of learning objectives.
- **Materials Required**—Every lab includes information on hardware, software, and other materials you will need to complete the lab.
- **Completion Times**—Every lab has an estimated completion time so that you can plan your activities more accurately.
- **Activity Sections**—Labs are presented in manageable sections. Where appropriate, additional Activity Background information is provided to illustrate the importance of a particular project.
- **Step-by-Step Instructions**—Every lab provides steps to enhance technical proficiency; some labs include Critical Thinking exercises to challenge students.
- **Review Questions**—Some labs include review questions to help reinforce concepts presented in the lab.

SOFTWARE REQUIREMENTS

- Computer running Windows 98, Windows Me, Windows 2000, or Windows XP
- Java 2 Platform, Standard Edition, v 1.4.1, which you can download from *http://java.sun.com*

COMPLETING THE LAB ASSIGNMENTS

Some lab assignments require written answers to complete an exercise, while others are programming assignments that require you to work with a Java compiler.

- To complete the written assignments, remove the pages that your instructor assigns, and then write your answers directly on the pages of the Lab Manual.

- To complete the programming assignments, use the compiler that your instructor recommends or requires. Print all the documentation assigned, including program code, program prompts, input, and output displayed on the screen, input files, and output files. You can submit your written answers and the printed documentation with a lab cover sheet for grading.

  If your instructor requires an electronic copy of your work, e-mail the completed assignment to your instructor or include a floppy disk with your work. Your instructor will tell you what is needed, but be sure to submit the .java, .class, and any .dat or .txt files that you create, as well as any input and output files. Also include your name or ID in the titles of all your files.

- To provide program documentation, compile and run your program, copy the prompts, input, and output (if appropriate), and paste them as a block comment at the end of your program.

  In Windows 2000, click the Mark button on the toolbar of the output window. (The toolbar appears by default; if the output window does not have a toolbar, follow the instructions for Windows XP.) Drag to select the text you want to copy, and then click the Copy button. Open your program in a text editor, click at the end of the program, and type /* to begin a block comment. Press Ctrl+V to paste the text in the program file, and then type */ to end the block comment.

  In Windows XP, right-click the title bar of the output window, point to Edit, and then click Mark. Drag to select the text you want to copy, and then press Enter. Open your program in a text editor, click at the end of the program, and type /* to begin a block comment. Press Ctrl+V to paste the text in the program file, and then type */ to end the block comment.

  After you paste the comment in the program, either print the program file from your text editor or submit the program file to your instructor electronically.

ABOUT THE AUTHOR

Judy Scholl has been a Professor of Computer Science at Austin Community College in Austin, Texas since 1988. She currently teaches programming languages and Web authoring courses. She received her Ph.D. from the University of Texas at Austin.

ACKNOWLEDGMENTS

To my good friend, David Orshalick, who always encouraged me to pursue writing.

I would like to thank the reviewers for the endless hours they spent reviewing my chapters, including Craig Murray of Indiana University Purdue University at Indianapolis, Ray Gill of Anne Arundel Community College, and Khaled Mansour of Washtenaw Community College. I would also like to thank Vitaly Davidovich and Thomas Pedrick, QA testers, and especially Lisa Ruffolo, Developmental Editor and Jennifer Muroff, Senior Editor, and Alyssa Pratt, Project Manager, for their patience and help. A special thanks to Dick Baldwin, Jack Jackson, Bill Tucker, Milton Gatewood, and Gerry Hamilton for technical support. Without the support of my husband, Jack, and my children Jenny, Jeremy, Joni, and Jaime, I could never have completed this project.

AN OVERVIEW OF COMPUTERS AND PROGRAMMING LANGUAGES

In this chapter, you will:

♦ Learn about different types of computers

♦ Explore the hardware and software components of a computer system

♦ Learn about the language of a computer

♦ Learn about the evolution of programming languages

♦ Examine high-level programming languages

♦ Discover what a compiler is and what it does

♦ Examine how a Java program is processed

♦ Learn what an algorithm is and explore problem-solving techniques

♦ Become aware of structured design and object-oriented design programming methodologies

CHAPTER 1: ASSIGNMENT COVER SHEET

Name _____   Date _____

Section _____

Lab Assignments	Grade
Lab 1.1 Identifying Different Types of Computers	
Lab 1.2 Identifying and Defining Hardware and Software Components	
Lab 1.3 Storing Information Electronically	
Lab 1.4 Processing a Java Program	
Lab 1.5 Programming with the Problem Analysis-Coding-Execution Cycle	
Lab 1.6 Object-Oriented Programming	
Total Grade	

See your instructor or the introduction to this book for instructions on submitting your assignments.

LAB 1.1 IDENTIFYING DIFFERENT TYPES OF COMPUTERS

Computers have evolved from their introduction in the 1950s, when there were very few computers, through the 1960s, when manufacturers produced very large, expensive computers, to the 1970s, when people began to use cheaper, smaller computers. Today computers are affordable and faster. Regardless of the type, mainframe, midsize, and microcomputers share basic elements, including input, output, storage, and performance of arithmetic and logical operations.

A mainframe computer was once one of the largest, fastest, and most powerful computers available. However, a mainframe in 1960 was less powerful than today's microcomputer. A midsize computer was less expensive, less powerful, and smaller than a mainframe, and was created as a more affordable alternative to mainframes. Today the microcomputer is called the personal computer. Personal computers are usually sold with descriptions of their features printed on their cases to help non-specialist consumers match the features with their needs.

Objectives

In this lab, you become acquainted with the different types of computers that have evolved and identify how these types are used.

After completing this lab, you will be able to:

- Identify and define the different types of computers.

- Identify the different uses of the different types of computers.

Estimated completion time: **10–15 minutes**

Identifying Different Types of Computers

Match the following terms with the appropriate definitions.

1. _____ 1950s

2. _____ 1960s

3. _____ 1990s

4. _____ Mainframe

5. _____ Midsize computer

6. _____ Microcomputer

a) Personal computer

b) When computers became affordable for non-specialists

c) A computer less expensive and smaller than a mainframe that allowed more companies to afford computers

d) When computers were introduced to very few people

e) When large companies began to use computers

f) One of the largest, fastest, and most powerful computers until recently

LAB 1.2 IDENTIFYING AND DEFINING HARDWARE AND SOFTWARE COMPONENTS

A computer is made up of physical components (hardware) and programs (software). You should be able to identify these elements of a computer system and understand and define terminology used to describe a computer system.

Objectives

In this lab, you become acquainted with common computer terminology regarding hardware and software components.

After completing this lab, you will be able to:

- Identify and define hardware components.

- Distinguish between types of programs.

- Recognize addressing, storage, input, and output.

> Estimated completion time: **15–20 minutes**

Identifying and Defining Hardware Components

Match the following terms with the appropriate definitions.

1. _____ Accumulator

    a) An electronic device that can perform commands to input, output, or store data, and can calculate arithmetic and logical expressions

2. _____ Address

    b) Computer components including the central processing unit (CPU), main memory (MM), input/output devices, and secondary storage

3. _____ Arithmetic logic unit

    c) The brain of the computer, containing several components such as the control unit (CU), program counter (PC), instruction register (IR), arithmetic logic unit (ALU), and accumulator (ACC)

4. _____ Computer

    d) Controls a program's overall execution

5. _____ CPU

    e) Points to the next instruction to be executed

6. _____ CU

    f) Holds the instruction that is currently being executed

7. _____ Hardware

    g) Holds the results of the operations performed by the arithmetic logic unit

8. _____ Input devices

    h) The component of the CPU that performs arithmetic and logical operations

9. _____ Instruction register

    i) A unique location in main memory

10. _____ Output devices

    j) Stores information permanently

11. _____ Program counter

    k) Devices including keyboard, mouse, and secondary storage

12. _____ Secondary storage

    l) Devices including monitor, printer, and secondary storage

Identifying and Defining Software Components

Match the following terms with the appropriate definitions.

1. _____ Application program
2. _____ Program
3. _____ Software
4. _____ System program

a) Computer instructions to solve a problem

b) There are two types: system and application

c) Controls the computer

d) Performs a specific task; examples include word processors, spreadsheets, and games

Answer questions about the computer you use in your computer lab:

1. What is the operating system of the computer you use?

2. How much memory does the computer you use have?

3. What type of CPU does the computer you use have?

4. How much secondary storage does the computer you use have?

LAB 1.3 STORING INFORMATION ELECTRONICALLY

A computer is an electronic device that processes digital signals, which represent information with a sequence of 0s and 1s—binary code. All data is stored and manipulated on a computer as binary code.

Objectives

In this lab, you become acquainted with electronic signals and the representative code used to interpret these signals.

After completing this lab, you will be able to:

- Identify machine representation of computer code.

Estimated completion time: **15–20 minutes**

Storing Information Electronically

Fill in each blank with the appropriate term.

1. The two types of electrical signals are _____ and _____.

2. _____ signals represent information with a sequence of 0s and 1s.

3. The instructions written using the actual digits 0 and 1 are used to represent _____.

4. The digits 0 and 1 are called _____ or the shortened term _____.

5. The sequence of 0s and 1s is referred to as _____.

6. A sequence of eight bits is called a(n) _____.

7. The most common text-encoding scheme on personal computers is _____ _____ and is abbreviated as _____.

8. The character represented by the decimal number 97 is _____.

9. The character represented by the decimal number 65 is _____.

10. Java differentiates between uppercase and lowercase characters. True or false? _____

11. Early computers using machine language that used binary code made programming prone to errors. True or false? _____

12. Assembly language used _____ to make instruction easy to remember.

13. A program that translates assembly language instructions into machine language is called a(n) _____.

14. A program that translates instructions written in a high-level language into machine code is called a(n) _____.

Give the decimal representations of the following integers and characters:

1. 'A'   _____
2. 4   _____
3. '4'   _____
4. 'a'   _____
5. '\n'   _____
6. '\0'   _____
7. 0   _____
8. '0'   _____

LAB 1.4 PROCESSING A JAVA PROGRAM

Java is one of many programming languages that are high-level languages, which makes it closer to a natural language than machine language and assembly language. To run on a computer, Java instructions first need to be translated into an intermediate language called bytecode and then interpreted into a particular machine language. A program called a compiler translates instructions written in Java into bytecode. Java programs are machine independent, meaning that they can run on many different types of computer platforms.

There are two types of Java programs—applications and applets. Four steps are necessary to execute a program written in Java.

- You use an editor to create a program that is called the source program. The program must be saved in a text file named *ClassName*.java where *ClassName* is the name of the Java class contained in the file.

- The program is checked by another program called a compiler to check for syntax errors. When the program is syntactically correct, the compiler translates the program into bytecode and saves it in a file with the .class extension.

- To run a Java application program, the .class file must be loaded into the computer memory. To run a Java applet program, you must use a Web browser or applet viewer. These steps use a specific program that is part of a software development kit (SDK) containing several programs, or libraries, which perform a specific application that leads to creating an executable program. You must bring the code for the resources that you use from the SDK into your program to produce a final program that the computer can execute. A Java library is organized into a set of packages where each package contains a collection of related classes. A program called linker links the bytecode of your program with the library code.

- To execute the Java program, the linked code needs to be loaded in the main memory. This requires a program called a loader. A program called an interpreter translates each bytecode instruction into the machine language of your computer, and then executes it.

Objectives

In this lab, you become acquainted with the different programs in the SDK that are needed to process a source program written in a high-level language program.

After completing this lab, you will be able to:

- Identify the process needed to convert a high-level language program to an executable program.

Estimated completion time: **10–15 minutes**

Processing a Java Program

Match the following terms with the appropriate definitions.

1. _____ Alternative names for linking

   a) The program used to create a program in a high-level language

2. _____ Applications and applets

   b) The program created using an editor that follows the rules or syntax of a high-level language

3. _____ Compiler

   c) Two types of Java programs

4. _____ Editor

   d) The program that checks for correctness of syntax and translates a program into machine language

5. _____ Library

   e) A set of programs to help write a high-level program that produces a final executable program

6. _____ Linker

   f) The location of prewritten code used as a resource with the source code that has been successfully compiled

7. _____ Loader

   g) A program that combines the bytecode with other programs provided by the SDK and used in the program to create the executable code

8. _____ Programs contained in an SDK

   h) A program that loads an executable program into main memory

9. _____ Software Development Kit (SDK)

   i) An editor, compiler, linker, and loader

10. _____ Source program

   j) Build, rebuild, and make

LAB 1.5 PROGRAMMING WITH THE PROBLEM ANALYSIS-CODING-EXECUTION CYCLE

To become a good programmer, you must learn good problem-solving techniques. To develop a program to solve a problem, you start by analyzing a problem, outlining the problem requirements, and designing steps, called an algorithm, to solve the problem. Next, you implement the algorithm in a programming language. You follow the four steps listed in Lab 1.4 to run the program and verify that the algorithm works. Lastly, you maintain the program by using and modifying it if the problem domain changes.

Running a program successfully does not necessarily mean that the program runs correctly. You need to test your program with sample data to check whether it runs correctly. If it does not, you must examine the code, the algorithm, or even the problem analysis.

Dividing a problem into smaller subproblems is called structured design. In structured design, you analyze a subproblem, and then produce a solution for the subproblem. The process of implementing a structured design is called structured programming, or top-down design, stepwise refinement, and modular programming.

Objectives

In this lab, you learn problem solving and design steps to solve problems.

After completing this lab, you will be able to:

- Analyze problems and produce the steps necessary to solve the problem.

Estimated completion time: **45 minutes**

Programming with the Problem Analysis-Coding-Execution Cycle

Answer the following questions or complete the steps for problem solving.

1. What are the three steps required in problem solving in the programming environment?

2. Insert the problem analysis-coding-execution cycle steps in following steps. Include arrows that indicate the flow when an error occurs and when there is no error.

```
                    ┌──────────────┐
                    │   Problem    │
                    └──────────────┘

                    ┌──────────────┐
                    │              │
                    └──────────────┘

                    ┌──────────────┐
                    │              │
                    └──────────────┘

                    ┌──────────────┐
                    │              │          (Use Editor)
                    └──────────────┘

                    ┌──────────────┐
                    │   Compiler   │
    ┌──────────┐    └──────────────┘
    │ Library  │    ┌──────────────┐
    └──────────┘    │    Linker    │
                    └──────────────┘

                    ┌──────────────┐
                    │    Loader    │
                    └──────────────┘

                    ┌──────────────┐
                    │  Execution   │
                    └──────────────┘

                    ┌──────────────┐
                    │              │
                    └──────────────┘
```

3. What is the most important step in program development? Why?

4. What are three other names used to represent structured design? What is the basis for structured design?

5. Once a problem has been divided into subproblems, what step must occur next?

6. Converting your design into a high-level language only occurs after your design has been checked to be logically sound. What steps do you take once you have created your source code from your design?

7. Even if a program executes successfully, how do you know that it is correct?

8. Consider the problem of converting miles to kilometers. To find the equivalent kilometers, the number of miles is divided by 0.62. Write the algorithm to find the number of kilometers equivalent to the number of miles input.

LAB 1.6 OBJECT-ORIENTED PROGRAMMING

In contrast to structured design programming, a methodology called object-oriented design (OOD) starts solving problems by identifying objects and then determining how the objects interact with one another. A programming language that uses OOD is called an object-oriented programming (OOP) language.

Each object consists of data and operations on those data combined into a single unit. To create operations, you write algorithms and implement them in a programming language. You use methods to implement algorithms. In Java, the mechanism that allows you to combine data and operations on the data into a single unit is called a class. Java was designed especially to implement OOD. Furthermore, OOD works well and is used in conjunction with structured design.

Objectives

In this lab, you learn how to solve problems using the object-oriented design methodology.

After completing this lab, you will be able to:

- Identify objects and the relevant data and possible operations performed on that data.

Estimated completion time: **15–20 minutes**

Object-Oriented Programming

Answer the following questions or complete the steps for solving problems.

Identifying objects or components is the first step in problem solving in OOD. Consider Example 1-2 on page 13 of the text book as an OOD design rather than a structured programming design.

1. What are the objects?

2. For each object, specify some possible relevant data and possible operations to be performed on that data.

2

BASIC ELEMENTS OF JAVA

In this chapter, you will:

♦ Become familiar with the basic components of a Java program, including methods, special symbols, and identifiers

♦ Explore primitive data types

♦ Discover how to use arithmetic operators

♦ Examine how a program evaluates arithmetic expressions

♦ Explore how mixed expressions are evaluated

♦ Learn type casting

♦ Become familiar with the String type

♦ Learn what an assignment statement is and what it does

♦ Discover how to input data into memory using input statements

♦ Become familiar with the use of increment and decrement operators

♦ Examine ways to output results using output statements

♦ Learn how to import packages and why they are necessary

♦ Discover how to create a Java application program

♦ Explore how to properly structure a program, including using comments to document a program

CHAPTER 2: ASSIGNMENT COVER SHEET

Name _____   Date _____

Section _____

Lab Assignments	Grade
Lab 2.1 Identifying Basic Elements of a Java Program	
Lab 2.2 Identifying Data Types	
Lab 2.3 Using Arithmetic Operators	
Lab 2.4 Using the class String	
Lab 2.5 Allocating Memory, Writing Assignment Statements, and Writing Input Statements	
Lab 2.6 Using Strings, Writing to the Screen, Using Common Escape Sequences, and Using the Method flush	
Lab 2.7 Using Packages, Classes, Methods, and the Import Statement to Write a Java Program using Good Programming Style and Form (Critical Thinking Exercises)	
Total Grade	

See your instructor or the introduction to this book for instructions on submitting your assignments.

LAB 2.1 IDENTIFYING BASIC ELEMENTS OF A JAVA PROGRAM

A computer program is a sequence of statements whose objective is to accomplish a task. Recall that there are two types of Java programs—applications and applets. In this book, you start with Java application programs. To write meaningful programs, you must learn the special symbols, words, and syntax rules of any programming language. You must also learn semantic rules, which determine the meaning of the instructions. Additionally, you should learn the tokens, which are the smallest units of a program written in any programming language. Java tokens are divided into special symbols, word symbols, and identifiers.

Following are some special symbols in Java:

+	–	*	/
.	;	?	,
<=	!=	==	>=

Some word symbols (reserved words or keywords) in Java are `int`, `float`, `double`, `char`, `void`, `public`, `static`, `throws`, and `return`.

Identifiers are simply names. Some identifiers are predefined; others are defined by the user. A Java identifier can only consist of letters, digits, the underscore character (_), and the dollar sign character ($). Identifiers cannot start with a digit and are case sensitive. Although identifiers can be of any length, each computer system sets a maximum for the number of significant characters it processes, which restricts the length of an identifier.

Objectives

In this lab, you become acquainted with tokens, which are the special symbols, word symbols, and identifiers used in Java statements.

After completing this lab, you will be able to:

- Recognize special symbols.
- Recognize word symbols.
- Recognize identifiers.
- Recognize invalid symbol representations.

Estimated completion time: **15–20 minutes**

Identifying Basic Elements of a Java Program

Indicate whether each of the following representations is a special symbol, word symbol, identifier, or is invalid.

Token	Special symbol	Word symbol	Identifier	Invalid
1. ABC				
2. xy!				
3. double				
4. $2ft				
5. &&ab				
6. ab*				
7. return				
8. c3po				
9. void				
10. 123z				
11. FLOAT				
12. date				
13. qr&				
14. first name				
15. *				
16. R2D2				
17. 5day				
18. !=				
19. +xy				
20. hello				

LAB 2.2 IDENTIFYING DATA TYPES

Java categorizes data into different types, and only certain operations can be performed on particular types of data. Every data type is associated with a different set of values. The data type also determines the amount of memory used, and consequently, how a value or other data is represented. A data type is a set of values together with a set of operations.

The primitive data types are the fundamental data types in Java. Primitive data type categories include integral, floating-point, and Boolean. Integral types are integers or numbers without a decimal point. Floating-point types are decimal numbers. Boolean types are logical values.

Integral data types are further classified into five categories: char, byte, short, int, and long. Each type is associated with a different set of values. This chapter focuses on int, Boolean, and char data types.

Positive integers do not need a plus (+) sign in front of them. No commas are used with an integer. The char data type is used to represent single characters such as letters, digits, and special symbols. The char data type can represent every key on your keyboard and every printable character. When using the char data type, you enclose each character represented within single quotation marks.

Java uses the Unicode character set, which contains 65,536 values numbered 0 to 65,535. Another common character data set is the American Standard Code for Information Interchange (ASCII), which has 128 values. The first 128 characters of Unicode are the same as the characters in ASCII. Each character has a predefined order, which is called a collating sequence. The collating sequence is used when you compare characters.

The Boolean data type has only two values: true and false. The central purpose of the Boolean type is to manipulate logical (Boolean) expressions.

The floating-point data type is represented in the form of scientific notation called floating-point notation. Java has two data types to represent numbers with decimals. The data type float uses 4 bytes, which holds numbers between −3.4E+38 and 3.4E+38, and has a maximum number of significant digits of six or seven. The data type double uses 8 bytes, holds numbers between −1.7E+308 and 1.7E+308, and has a maximum number of significant digits of fifteen. The maximum number of significant digits is called precision. For your lab exercises in this workbook, you usually use the double type instead of the float type.

Objectives

In this lab, you become acquainted with the primitive data type categories integral, floating-point, and Boolean.

After completing this lab, you will be able to:

- Identify the primitive data type categories integral, floating-point, and Boolean.

Estimated completion time: **15–20 minutes**

Identifying Data Types

Identify which primitive data type could be used to represent the value.

Value	Integral	Floating	Boolean	Character	Invalid
1. −2147483648					
2. true					
3. 1					
4. 0					
5. '?'					
6. −654.78					
7. '123'					
8. '1'					
9. 66					
10. 7.8E3					
11. 0.1E-6					
12. ''					
13. ' '					
14. '+'					
15. int					
16. "false"					
17. +36					
18. 0.0					
19. 127.0					
20. false					

LAB 2.3 USING ARITHMETIC OPERATORS

Computer programming uses five arithmetic operators: + (addition), − (subtraction), * (multiplication), / (division), and % (remainder, or modulus operator). Arithmetic expressions and precedence are evaluated as they are in mathematics; however, the symbols—the operators—used in evaluation have minor differences. For instance, in mathematics "a times b" can be written as a × b, ab, a(b) (a)b, or (a)(b). In Java "a times b" can only be written using the * operator. Parentheses can be used, such as a*b, (a*b), or (a)*(b), but they do not indicate multiplication.

The numbers or variables in the expression are called operands. Operators that have two operands are called binary operators. Operators that have only one operand are called unary operators. When evaluated, mixed expressions with mixed operands change integers to floating-point numbers. Additionally, you can use the cast operator to explicitly convert data types.

Integer division truncates the result. For example, in integer division the expression 5/2 results in 2 (with no decimal). In floating point division the expression 5.0/2.0 results in 2.5. In a mixed expression of either 5/2.0 or 5.0/2 the result is 2.5.

The modulus operator works with integers to find the whole number remainder. Using the same example 5%2, the remainder is 1, not 0.5. The remainder of 3/4 is 3, not 0.75.

The operators *, /, and % have the same level of precedence, meaning that the operation occurs as it is encountered, left to right (unless overridden by parentheses), when evaluating the expression. The operators + and − have the same level of precedence, and that level is below the level of the operators *, /, and %.

Because the char data type is also an integral data type, Java allows you to perform arithmetic operations on char data. The character '8' is different from the integer 8. While the integer value of 8 is 8, the integer value of the character '8' is 56.

A value of one data type can automatically change to another data type, as in a mixed expression. This process is called implicit type coercion. To avoid implicit type coercion, Java provides for explicit type conversion through the use of the cast operator, also called type conversion or type casting. Type casting does not change the actual value of a variable, but only the value of an expression.

Objectives

In this lab, you learn the mathematical representation in Java of arithmetic expressions and precedence. Additionally, you learn to evaluate expressions using type conversion (casting).

After completing this lab, you will be able to:

- Evaluate arithmetic expressions using addition, subtraction, multiplication, division, and remainder.
- Use type conversion (casting) in arithmetic evaluations.
- Evaluate arithmetic expressions by precedence.
- Evaluate mixed arithmetic expressions.

Estimated completion time: **20-30 minutes**

Using Arithmetic Operators

Evaluate the following expressions or indicate that they are invalid if an illegal operator is used with the incorrect operand:

Expression	Result
1. 20 % (4 - 2)	
2. 20 / 4.0 * 6.4 / 2	
3. 4 % 5	
4. 3.0 * (6 / 24)	
5. 3 – (3 + 3.0) * 10 / 3	
6. 12.0 % 4	
7. 7 * 6 / 21 / 3.0	
8. 11 % 4 * 3.0	
9. 17 % 4 / 3	
10. 5 % 6 / 4	
11. 5 / 4.0 * 5	
12. 6 + 2 / 4	
13. (2 - 3 + (2 * (3 / 3) % 1))	
14. 5 % 4	
15. 5 – (2.0 + 5) * 10 / 2	
16. (double)(4)/3	
17. (int)(3.7)+5.3	
18. (int)(3.7+5.3)	
19. (double)(5/2)	
20. (char)(65)	

LAB 2.4 USING THE `class` STRING

Values that contain more than one character are called strings and use the class name String. However, strictly speaking, a string is a sequence of zero or more characters, and strings are not a primitive type. A string with no characters is called a null or empty string. In Java, strings are enclosed in double quotation marks. To process strings effectively, Java provides the class String, which contains various operations to manipulate a string.

Every character in a string has a relative position in the string. The position of the first character is 0, the position of the second character is 1, and so on. The length of a string is the number of characters in it. Remember that a space is a character.

If a string is a numeric string, meaning that it consists of only integers or decimal values, then the string must be converted into numeric form to perform numeric operations. To convert a string to an integer, use the expression Integer.parseInt(strExpression). To convert a string to a float, use the expression Float.parseFloat(strExpression) or Double.parseDouble(strExpression).

Objectives

In this lab, you learn to convert string expressions to integer, float, and double expressions.

After completing this lab, you will be able to:

- Convert string expressions to integer, float, and double expressions.

Estimated completion time: **15–20 minutes**

Using the class string

Convert the following String expressions to their equivalent numeric form.

String expression	Method to convert to the equivalent numeric form
1. "64.592"	
2. "–64.592"	
3. "2"	
4. Multiply "5" times "50"	
5. Multiply "5.0" times "50"	
6. Subtract "5.8" from "10"	
7. Modulus of "5" by "3"	
8. Divide "5" by "3"	
9. Add "6.2" to "5.1"	
10. Add "6.2" to "5"	

LAB 2.5 ALLOCATING MEMORY, WRITING ASSIGNMENT STATEMENTS, AND WRITING INPUT STATEMENTS

When you allocate memory, you use a name to identify each memory location being allocated. Additionally, you indicate the type of data that will be stored in those memory locations. A memory location whose value cannot be changed is called a named constant. It is customary to use all uppercase characters for memory location identifiers (names) that are named constants. Using uppercase characters for named constants is not required, but does set constants apart from memory locations whose values can be changed. Named constants do not change their values and must be initialized at declaration. You declare a memory location as a named constant with the following syntax:

static final *dataType identifier = value*;

In Java, `static` and `final` are reserved words. The word `final` specifies that the value stored in the memory location is fixed and cannot be changed. The word `static` is optional, depending on the circumstance.

In Java, memory locations that can be changed are called variable memory locations or variables. Variables can be initialized at declaration and can be given different values throughout execution. You declare a variable with the following syntax:

dataType identifier1, identifier2, …, identifierN;

Data is stored in variables either through an assignment statement or through an input (read) statement. Assignment statements use the = assignment operator. Java evaluates the expression to the right of the assignment operator, and stores the result in the memory address identified by the variable to the left of the operator. The result of the expression on the right must be a value compatible with the data type of the variable on the left. The first time a value is placed in the variable is called initialization. Tracing values through a sequence of statements, called a walk-through or desk checking, is a valuable tool to learn and practice.

In Java, using a variable without initializing it causes a compile time error unless the variable is a class field; in this case the default value is automatically assigned to the variable.

When the computer receives data from the keyboard, the user is said to be acting interactively. In Java, you insert data into variables from the standard input device by using the standard input stream object, System.in. Data is extracted in the form of character bytes from the input stream. Input in Java is limited to character and string input. To read characters from the input stream, you declare and initialize an input stream variable as follows:

```
InputStreamReader charReader = new InputStreamReader(System.in);
```

To read an entire line of characters, you declare and initialize another input stream variable as follows:

```
BufferedReader keyboard = new BufferedReader(charReader);
```

This statement declares the keyboard to be a BufferedReader variable. This variable is initialized to the standard input device using the variable charReader. Accordingly, charReader and keyboard are input stream objects. Data can be input and assigned to a string object, and then parsed into numeric data when necessary, or it can be parsed and input in one statement and assigned to a numeric variable. To read a single character, you can use the method read and the cast operator to convert the character to an integer value, if necessary.

Variables can obtain values either through input or through assignment. Inputting data offers the program more flexibility and requires a prompt to the user to enter the data. Assignments are used in calculations. The increment and decrement operators are used in assignment statements or with the variable name alone to increase or decrease a variable by one.

Objectives

In this lab, you learn that allocating memory with both variables and named constants results in the program assigning a name and type to the memory location. You must initialize named constants when you declare them; initialization is optional for variables. Additionally, you learn that the value of variables can be changed through assignment or inputting data. When changing a variable by the value 1, you can use increment and decrement operators.

After completing this lab, you will be able to:

- Allocate memory with both variables and named constants.

- Assign values to variables when expressions are evaluated.

- Assign values to variables through input.

- Use the decrement and increment operators.

Estimated completion time: **30 minutes**

Allocating Memory, Writing Assignment Statements, and Writing Input Statements

Describe the following declarations, assignments, and input statements. Indicate the value in memory after each statement is executed. Write "invalid" if the statement is not executable.

Statement	Show the variable name and value of each statement
1. int a, b = 9; a = b;	
2. int d = 2, x = 3, y = 1; y + 4 = d - x;	
3. short number = 10; number = 0;	

4. short number = 0;
   number = 10;
   number = number + 5;
   number = (short)(number + 5);
   What occurs if your statement is:
   number = (number + 5);	

5. double value = 12.0;
   value = 10.0;
   value = value + 0.5;	

6. final int b = 9;	

7. double x = -14.5, y = 22.5;
   int d = 3;
   y = d - x + y;	

8. double ans = 4;	

9. int n;
   String nstring;
   // The user should be asked for a value here.
   // Assume the user enters 3.
   nstring = keyboard.readLine();
   n = Integer.parseInt(nstring);	

Statement	Show the variable name and value of each statement

10. char a;
    // The user should be asked for a value here.
    // Assume the user enters 'b'.
    a = (char) keyboard.read();	

11. double x;
    // The user should be asked for a value here.
    // Assume the user enters 3.24.
    x = Double.parseDouble(keyboard.readLine());	

12. double a, b, c = 0.0;	
13. int d = 2, x = 3, y = 4; 4 = d − x + y;	
14. double def = 123.5; int y; y = def;	
15. int b = 9.0;	

16. int num1= 8, num2 = 3, temp = 0;
    temp = num1;
    num1 = num2;
    num2 = temp;	

17. int num;
    // The user should be asked for a value here.
    // Assume the user enters 8.
    num = Integer.parseInt(keyboard.readLine());
 	
    num++;	

18. int c = 8;
    ++c;
    c--;	

19. double x = 5.0;
    int y = 4;
    x = x + y / 4;	

20. double x = 5.0;
    int y = 4;
    y = x + y/4;	

Lab 2.6 Using Strings, Writing to the Screen, Using Common Escape Sequences, and Using the Method flush

When used with numerics, the + operator adds numeric values. When used with two strings, a string and a character, or a string and a numeric, the + operator concatenates the two.

In Java, you produce output on the standard output device, System.out. You can use two methods, print and println, to output a string on the standard output device. These form output statements. The expression of the output statement is evaluated and its value is printed at the current cursor position on the output device. The method print leaves the cursor after the last character of the expression. The method println positions the cursor at the beginning of the next line. You can use the newline escape sequence '\n' to move the cursor to the beginning of the next line. The '\n' can be written as a character by itself or within a string. When writing a print or println statement, you can wrap the instruction from one line to another without closing the string and reopening it on the next line. You can use the + concatenation operator to continue an output statement on the next line. If you break a string in a sentence, remember to include blanks between the last word of the first string and the first word of the next string.

Some escape sequences to control the output are more common than others. In addition to the newline, '\n', the tab, '\t', moves the cursor to the next tab stop, the backspace, '\b', moves the cursor one space to the left, the return, '\r', moves the cursor to the beginning of the current line (not the next line), the backslash '\\', allows a backslash to be printed, the single quotation, '\'', allows the single quotation to be printed, and the double quotation, '\"', allows the double quotation to be printed.

Output generated by the method print first goes into an area of the computer called a buffer. When the buffer is full, the output is sent to the output device. The method println empties the buffer even when the buffer is not full. You can use the method flush, which is associated with the System.out, to empty the buffer even if it is not full. However, the method flush does not automatically position the cursor at the beginning of the next line.

Objectives

In this lab, you learn to use the standard output object and the methods print and println to display expressions or manipulators on the screen.

After completing this lab, you will be able to:

- Display expressions on the screen.

- Use strings with strings, numerics, and characters.

- Use common escape sequences.

- Use the method flush.

Estimated completion time: **30–40 minutes**

Using Strings, Writing to the Screen, Using Common Escape Sequences, and Using the Method flush

Describe the following declarations, assignment, input, and output statements, or write Java code to implement the comment statements. Describe what is contained in memory and show what is displayed on the screen after each output statement is executed.

1. Describe what the program displays when it processes each of the following lines of code:

```
final double PI = 3.1416;
```

```
double radius = 2.5;
```

```
System.out.print("The area of the circle is " + PI * radius * radius.");
System.out.flush();
```

2. Write the appropriate Java statement to match the description in each of the following comments:

// declare an integer variable for the width of a rectangle

// declare an integer variable for the length of a rectangle

// prompt the user for the width of a rectangle

// input the width value

// prompt the user for the length of a rectangle

// input the length value

// output the area of the rectangle found by multiplying length times width

3. After each set of input and output statements, indicate the purpose of the code.

```
double balance;
double deposit;
double checks;
System.out.print("Enter your beginning checkbook balance: ");
balance = Double.parseDouble(keyboard.readLine());
    //assume 536.25 is entered
```

```
System.out.print("Enter your deposits for the month: ");
deposit = Double.parseDouble(keyboard.readLine());
    //assume 64.75 is entered
```

```
System.out.print("Enter your checks for the month: ");
checks = Double.parseDouble(keyboard.readLine());
    //assume 425.50 is entered
```

```
System.out.println("Your ending check balance is: " + (balance
    + deposit — checks))";
```

4. Write the appropriate Java statement to match the description in each of the following comments:

// declare four double variables called num1, num2, num3, and average

// ask the user to input the first value

// input the value into num1

// ask the user to input the second value

// input the value into num2

// ask the user to input the third value

// input the value into num3

// assign average the value of num1, num2, and num3 divided by 3.0

// output a statement with a message describing the values input and the average

5. When a value is assigned in memory, the value previously stored in memory is replaced by the new assigned value. This is called destructive replacement. If you want two memory locations to exchange values, you need to save a value in a third location to prevent losing the original value. The following code shows how to swap two values in memory. Explain the purpose of each of the following lines.

```
int num1 = 10, num2 = 5, temp;
```

```
System.out.println("num1 is " + num1 +", num2 is "+ num2);
```

```
temp = num1;
```

```
num1 = num2;
```

```
num2 = temp;
```

```
System.out.println("Now the numbers are swapped and num1 is " + num1 +
    ", num2 is " + num2);
```

6. Write the appropriate Java statements to match the descriptions in the following comments:

// declare two integer variables feet and inches

// ask the user how many feet tall they are (no fraction)

// input the value entered into the variable feet
// ask the user how many additional inches tall they are (no fraction)

// input the value entered into the variable inches

// assign inches the value of inches plus feet times 12

// output with an appropriate message the number of inches the person is tall

7. Write the output of the following code.

```java
int x = 2, y = 3, z = 5;
System.out.println("This is my report in columns\n"
    + "\n\t" + x + '\t' + x * x
    + "\n\t" + y + '\t' + y * y
    + "\n\t" + z + '\t' + z * z);
```

8. Write a Java statement to match the descriptions in the following comments:

    //output a message that is your name used in the possessive form

    // followed by the name of your favorite movie in double quotes

Lab 2.7 Using Packages, Classes, Methods, and the Import Statement to Write a Java Program using Good Programming Style and Form

Java provides a collection of related classes in libraries, called packages, with methods, operators, and identifiers needed to run a Java application or applet. You can think of a method as a set of instructions designed to accomplish a specific task. The package java.io contains classes for inputting data into a program and outputting the results of a program.

To indicate which package to use in a program, you use the import statement, the package name, and the specific name of the class from the package that you need, separated from the package name by the dot operator and end the statement with a semicolon. For example, `importjava.io.*;` is an import statement.

A Java program, called source code, consists of a collection of classes from import statements and classes the programmer writes. The predefined methods parseInt, read, readLine, print, and println are provided as part of the system. In a Java application program, one method must be called main. The syntax of the main method definition may include a `throws` clause that addresses an undesirable situation, called an exception, which can be detected during program execution that the system cannot tolerate. Source code must be saved in a file with the extension .java. Moreover, the name of the class and the name of the file containing the Java program must be the same.

The method main must follow syntax, or grammar rules, and consists of a heading and the body. The statements are in the body and are enclosed in curly braces. Declaration statements are used to declare elements such as variables. Executable statements perform calculations, manipulate data, create output, accept input, and so on. Java programs follow not only Java syntax but also semantics, which is the set of rules that apply to the statements and operations. For ease of use, programs should be well documented both with comments and meaningful identifier names, and have an easy-to-read format. Use comments to document a program and explain its purpose, identify who wrote the program, and explain the purpose of particular statements. A single-line comment begins with // anywhere in the line. Everything encountered on that line after // is ignored by the compiler. Multiple-line comments are enclosed between /* and */.

Using meaningful identifier names is another way to document the program. Although not required for a program to run, use lowercase letters for variable names, uppercase letters for constant names, begin a class name with an uppercase letter, and join multiple words for a name using the underscore character '_'. For example, a typical variable name is hat_size or hatSize, while a typical constant name is CIRCLE_RADIUS. The examples in this book follow these standards. Another documentation tool is to provide clearly written prompts to inform the user how to interact correctly with a program.

In addition to simple assignment statements, you can use a compound assignment statement for more concise notation. The compound operators are +=, -=, *=, /=, and %=.

Objectives

In this lab, you learn to write complete programs with Java import statements.

After completing this lab, you will be able to:

- Read a complete program and determine the output.
- Write a complete program including import statements for input/output and strings.
- Use a readable format in a Java program.
- Use meaningful identifiers.
- Use comments for documentation.

Estimated completion time: **60–80 minutes**

Using Packages, Classes, Methods, and the Import Statement to Write a Java Program Using Good Programming Style and Form

Describe the following program declarations, assignments, input, and output statements. Indicate the value in memory after each statement is executed. Show what is displayed after each output statement or write Java code to implement the comment statements or program design. Use an editor to enter the programs. From the command line, compile and execute the programs. Then compare your work to the actual output of your programs.

1. Describe the following program, including the use of import statements when necessary. Show what is displayed as output. Enter and execute the program and name it **StuInfo1.java**. Save the source code in the Chap02 folder on your Student Disk.

   To compile your program from the command line, type **javac** followed by the name of your program using the .java extension, as in **javac StuInfo1.java**. Correct any errors until your program compiles.

   To execute your program from the command line, type **java** followed by the name of your program with no extension, as in **java StuInfo1**.

   After your program is executed, copy the output and save it in a block comment at the end of your program.

```java
import java.io.*;

public class StuInfo1
{

public static void main(String[] args) throws IOException
{
BufferedReader keyboard = new BufferedReader(new
InputStreamReader(System.in));

String first_name, last_name, classification, major;
double gpa;

System.out.print("Please enter your first name: ");
first_name=keyboard.readLine();

System.out.print("Please enter your last name: ");
last_name = keyboard.readLine();

System.out.print("Please enter your classification:\n"
 + "freshman, sophomore, junior, senior, special, or graduate: ");
classification = keyboard.readLine();

System.out.print("Please enter your major as an abbreviation: ");
major = keyboard.readLine();

System.out.print("Please enter your grade point average: ");
gpa = Double.parseDouble(keyboard.readLine());

System.out.println("\nYou have entered the following information:\n"
 + "\nName:\t\t" + first_name + ' ' + ' ' + last_name
 + "\nClassification:\t" + classification
 + "\nMajor:\t\t" + major
 + "\ngpa:\t\t" + gpa);
}
}
```

2. a. Design a Java program that prompts the user to select a lunch from several sandwich choices. The user should be prompted with the following information:

- Identification of the program and an explanation of how to use it

- Sandwich choices: Ham, Beef, Reuben, PBJ, Cheese, or Vegetarian

- Bread choices: Rye, Wheat, White, Sourdough, or Pumpernickel

- Condiment choices: Mayo, Mustard, Ketchup, or none

- Drink choices: Coke, Diet, Tea, Coffee, Water

- The price of a half sandwich or a whole sandwich: 3.99 or 5.99

Then the user enters his or her choice.

After all data has been entered, display the selection. Be sure to leave blank lines for readability, and include comments to identify the program author, to describe the program, and to describe program statements. You need the import statement for input and output. Use Lab 2.7, Exercise 1 as a guideline for designing the code.

Write your design in the following space. Your design should be a list of Java comments without any code.

2. b.   Write a Java program based on the design you created in Exercise 2a. Enter and execute the program and name it **Deli.java**. After your program is executed, copy the output and save it in a block comment at the end of your program. Save your source code in the Chap02 folder of your Student Disk.

Following is a copy of the screen results that might appear after running your program, depending on the data entered. The input entered by the user appears in bold.

```
Welcome to the Sandwich Corral

You will be given choices for building your sandwich.
Please enter your selection after each prompt and then press
the Enter key.

Please enter your sandwich choice.
Ham, Beef, Reuben, PBJ, Cheese, or Vegetarian: Ham
Please enter your bread selection.
Rye, Wheat, White, Sourdough, or Pumpernickel: Rye
Please enter your choice of condiment (one only).
Mayo, Mustard, Ketchup, none: Mustard
Please enter your drink choice.
Coke, Diet, Tea, Coffee, or Water: Water
Please enter 3.99 for a half sandwich or 5.99 for a whole
sandwich: 3.99

You have entered the following information:

Sandwich:      Ham
Bread:         Rye
Condiment:     Mustard
Drink:         Water

Tab:           3.99
```

3. a. *Critical Thinking Exercise*: Design a complete Java program that asks the user for two names. Display the two names the user enters—this is called echo printing. Swap the values of the names. For example, name1 will become name2, and name2 will become name1. Display the two names after they have been swapped. Use Lab 2.5, Exercise 16 for reference.

After all data has been entered and the names have been swapped, display the values of the names. Be sure to leave blank lines for readability and comments to identify the program author, to describe the program, and to describe program statements. You need the import statement for input and output.

Write your design in the following space. Your design should be a list of Java comments without any code.

3. b.   Write a Java program based on the design you created in Exercise 3a. Enter and execute the program, and then name it **Swap.java**. After your program is executed, copy the output and save it in a block comment at the end of your program. Save your source code in the Chap02 folder of your Student Disk.

Following is a copy of the screen results that might appear after running your program, depending on the data entered. The input entered by the user appears in bold.

```
You will be asked to enter two names.
The program will display the names you entered, swap
the names, and then display them after they are swapped.

Please enter the first name: Romeo
Please enter the second name: Juliet
You entered Romeo as your first name and Juliet as your
second name.


After swapping the names,
the first name is Juliet
and the second name is Romeo.
```

4. a.   *Critical Thinking Exercise*: Imagine that you are a real estate agent and make your living from sales commissions. House commissions paid to sell a house through multiple listings are 6% of the sales price. The listing agency receives 3% and the selling agency receives 3%. Of that 3%, each agency receives 1.5% and the selling agent or listing agent receives 1.5%. As a real estate agent, you want to know how much you will receive for a house that you either list or sell. For your records, identify the house by the owner's last name. Design a Java program that asks the user for the name and selling price of the home. Calculate the amount paid by the home owner to sell the home and the amount of the commission you will receive. Use a constant for the commission rates.

Write your design in the following space. Your design should be a list of Java comments without any code.

4. b.   Write a Java program based on the design you created in Exercise 4a. Enter the program, and then name it **Realtor.java**. After your program is executed, copy the output and save it in a block comment at the end of your program. Save your source code in the Chap02 folder of your Student Disk.

Following is a copy of the screen results that might appear after running your program, depending on the data entered. The input entered by the user appears in bold.

```
This program calculates the cost to sell a home
and the commission paid to an individual sales agent.

The user is asked for the last name of the seller and the
sales price.


Please enter owner's last name: Garcia
Please enter the sales price of the home: 100000


The Garcia's home sold for 100000.0
The cost to sell the home was 6000.0
The selling or listing agent earned 1500.0
```

INTRODUCTION TO OBJECTS AND INPUT/OUTPUT

In this chapter, you will:

♦ Learn about objects and reference variables

♦ Explore how to use predefined methods in a program

♦ Become familiar with the class String

♦ Learn how to use input and output dialog boxes in a program

♦ Learn how to tokenize the input stream

♦ Explore how to format the output of decimal numbers with the class DecimalFormat

♦ Become familiar with file input and output

CHAPTER 3: ASSIGNMENT COVER SHEET

Name _____   Date _____

Section _____

Lab Assignments	Grade
Lab 3.1 Examining Objects and Reference Variables, and Using the Predefined Class Math and the pow Method	
Lab 3.2 Using the String Class	
Lab 3.3 Using Dialog Boxes for Input and Output, Tokenizing Input Data, and Formatting Decimal Output (Critical Thinking Exercise)	
Lab 3.4 Using Files for Input and Output (Critical Thinking Exercise)	
Total Grade	

See your instructor or the introduction to this book for instructions on submitting your assignments.

LAB 3.1 EXAMINING OBJECTS AND REFERENCE VARIABLES, AND USING THE PREDEFINED CLASS MATH AND THE POW METHOD

In Chapter 2, you learned that the primitive data type allowed you to directly store data into its memory space. Other types of variables are reference variables that allow you to allocate memory for a variable, but not to directly store data in its memory space. The reference variable stores the memory location, that is, the address of the memory space where the actual data is stored. The value is stored by using the operator **new**, which is also a reserved word. In Java, any variable declared using a class is a reference variable. You declare a reference variable of the class by using the class name and the name of the variable. The memory space where the value is stored is called an object, or an instance of the class. Using the operator new to create a class object is called an instantiation of that class.

The method main executes automatically when you run a Java program. Other methods execute only when they are activated, or called. Classes included with the Java compiler are called predefined classes, which contain many useful predefined methods. To use a predefined class or a method, you need to know the name of the package, the name of the class, and the name of the method.

Methods in a class are either static or nonstatic. A static method can be called using the class and the object of the class. A nonstatic method is called using a reference variable of that class type. The expression used to activate a method is called a method call. Data is communicated between methods by the use of arguments or parameters. When a method is called, the data communicated is an argument. In the definition of the method, the data communicated uses a variable and called a parameter. The dot operator, called dot notation, is used to separate the class name from the member name, or method name.

The Java system contains the class Math in the package java.lang. One of the methods of the class Math is pow, which has two parameters to accept the base and exponent values and returns the value of the base raised to the exponent. Following are example statements that use the pow method:

```
numberRaised = math.pow(baseNumber, exponentNumber);
answer = answer + math.pow(baseNumber, exponentNumber) / 6.0 + 4;
```

Objectives

In this lab, you become acquainted with using the predefined method pow from the predefined class Math, using primitive data types and reference data types as arguments to the method pow.

After completing this lab, you will be able to:

- Use the predefined method pow from the predefined class Math found in the package java.lang.
- Use primitive data variables as arguments to the predefined method pow.
- Use reference data variables as arguments to the predefined method pow.

Estimated completion time: **40–50 minutes**

Examining Objects and Reference Variables, and Using the Predefined Class Math and the pow Method

Design and write complete Java programs based on the following instructions and output examples.

1. a. Design a Java program that asks the user to enter two integer values. Declare variables that are of the primitive data type. The first value is a base number; the second value is an exponent. Using the predefined method pow in the Math class, find the value of the base number raised to the exponent value. Display your values.

   Consider the following items in your design:

   - Input values

   - Output values

   - How you obtain your input values

   - How you calculate your output value

   - How you display your output value

   Write your design in the following space. Your design should be a list of Java comments without any code.

1. b.   Write a Java program based on the design you created in Exercise 1a. Enter the program, saving it as **Power1.java**. Then execute the program. Copy the output and save it according to your instructor's requirement. Text output can be saved in a block comment at the end of your program. Save your source code in the Chap03 folder of your Student Disk.

Following are copies of the text dialog boxes that may appear on the screen depending on the data the user enters. The input entered by the user appears in bold.

```
This program asks the user for two values.
The first value will be used as a base number, the second value
will be used as an exponent.


The program calculates the value of the base number raised
to the exponent number.


Please enter the base value: 4
Please enter the exponent value: 3


The value of 4.0 raised to the exponent 3.0 is 64.0
```

2. a.   Redesign your program from Lab 3.1, Exercise 1 using variables that are of the reference data type. *To display a reference variable, you must convert the variable to a primitive data type.* Use the object name, the dot operator and the method doubleValue, for example base.doubleValue().

Consider the following items in your design:

- Input values
- Output values
- How you obtain your input values
- How you calculate your output value
- How you display your output value

Write your design in the following space. Your design should be a list of Java comments without any code.

2. b. Write a Java program based on the design you created in Exercise 2a. Enter the program, saving it as **Power2.java**. Then execute the program. Copy the output and save it according to your instructor's requirement. Text output can be saved in a block comment at the end of your program. Save your source code in the Chap03 folder of your Student Disk.

Following are copies of screen results that might appear depending on the data the user enters. The input entered by the user appears in bold.

```
This program asks the user for two values.
The first value will be used as a base number, the second value
will be used as an exponent.


The program calculates the value of the base number raised
to the exponent number.


Please enter the base value: 4
Please enter the exponent value: 3

The value of 4.0 raised to the exponent 3.0 is 64.0
```

LAB 3.2 USING THE STRING CLASS

Each input to a program is a string. You must convert strings into numbers for processing. Before outputting numeric data, a Java program first converts numeric data into strings, which the program then displays or prints. When assigning a string value to a String variable, you are actually assigning a string value to a String object. String variables are reference variables. Java provides methods for string manipulations. The class String is part of the Java system. To use a String method you need to know its name, parameters, and what the method does.

A string is a sequence of zero or more characters. The position called the index, or the first character, is 0, the second character is 1, and so on. A String variable invokes a String method using the dot operator, the method name, and the set of arguments (if any) required by the method.

Objectives

In this lab, you learn to use methods of the String class.

After completing this lab, you will be able to use the following methods:

- String
- indexOf
- concat
- length
- substring
- toLowerCase
- toUpperCase

Estimated completion time: **50–60 minutes**

Using the String Class

Design and write complete Java programs based on the following instructions and output examples.

1. a. Design a Java program that assigns the string values "Hi" and "Hello World" to String variables. Display the following information:

    - Length of the string
    - Index of the character 'o'
    - Index of the next character 'o'
    - Concatenation of the string variable containing "Hi" with the substring containing "Hello World" beginning with the location of the character 'W'
    - String variable in all lowercase characters
    - String variable in all uppercase characters

    Write your design in the following space. Your design should be a list of Java comments without any code.

1. b.   Write a Java program based on the design you created in Exercise 1a. Enter the program, saving it as **Words.java**. Then execute the program. Copy the output and save it according to your instructor's requirement. Text output can be saved in a block comment at the end of your program. Save your source code in the Chap03 folder of your Student Disk.

Following are copies of screen results that might appear depending on the data the user enters.

```
This program demonstrates commonly used string methods.

The output displayed uses the string values "Hello World" and "Hi"

The length of the string "Hello World" is 11
The index of the first character 'o' in "Hello World" is 4
The index of the second character 'o' in "Hello World" is 7
The concatenation of Hi  and World is Hi World
The string value "Hello World" in all lowercase characters is hello
world
The string value "Hello World" in all uppercase characters is HELLO
WORLD
```

LAB 3.3 USING DIALOG BOXES FOR INPUT AND OUTPUT, TOKENIZING INPUT DATA, AND FORMATTING DECIMAL OUTPUT

In addition to the read, readLine, print, and println methods, Java provides input and output using a graphical user interface (GUI). This requires the use of the class JOptionPane contained in the package javax.swing and must be imported into the program. The showInputDialog method, with a string parameter, opens a dialog box containing the string parameter to prompt the user to enter data. The dialog box has a text field for the user to enter a string. The showMessageDialog method, with four parameters, opens a dialog box and controls the appearance of the dialog box. You use the boxTitleString parameter to create a title, the messageStringExpression to display a string expression, and the parameter messageType to display an icon. The parentComponent parameter is an object that represents the parent of the dialog box. When the parentComponent is the null value, the dialog box appears in the middle of the screen. When using a dialog box, the program must include the statement System.exit(0); to terminate properly.

In Chapter 2, all input required a separate read or readLine method for each data item read. Java contains the class StringTokenizer contained in the package java.io that allows multiple data items to be read from the input stream. Each data item, called a token, is separated by whitespace. To input multiple items of data you may want to declare a StringTokenizer object and a String object.

Following is an example of statements for tokenizing multiple data items from the keyboard:

```
String inputLine = keyboard.readLine();
StringTokenizer = new StringTokenizer(inputLine);
```

Following is an example that allows you to tokenize multiple data items from a dialog box:

```
inputLine = JOptionPane.showInputDialog("Message to the user.");
tokenizer = new StringTokenizer(inputLine);
```

By using format flags, you can format floating-point numbers to display decimal numbers in a specific manner using the method format from the class DecimalFormat. The format flags indicate the minimum number of digits to the left of the decimal point and the maximum number of digits to the right of the decimal point. The format flag 0 indicates that a digit should be displayed. The format flag # indicates that a space should appear if the digits are trailing zeros. Decimal numbers are rounded.

Objectives

In this lab, you become acquainted with using the dialog box for input and output, tokenizing input data, and formatting the output of decimal numbers.

After completing this lab, you will be able to:

- Input data through the dialog box.

- Output messages through the dialog box.

- Tokenize input data from the keyboard.

- Tokenize input data from the dialog box.

- Format the output of decimal numbers.

Estimated completion time: **60–90 minutes**

Using Dialog Boxes for Input and Output, Tokenizing Input Data, and Formatting Decimal Output

Write complete Java programs from the instructions and output examples given.

1. a. *Critical Thinking Exercise*: Redesign the program **Realtor.java**, which you stored in the Chap02 folder on your Student Disk. Use a dialog box to ask the user to enter the last name of the homeowner. Use another dialog box to ask the user to enter the selling price of the home. Use a third dialog box to display a message with the owner's name, the selling price of the home, the cost to the owner to sell the home, and the amount of the commission the selling agent will receive. Format the decimal output showing two decimal places.

    Write your design in the following space. Your design should be a list of Java comments without any code.

1. b. Write a Java program based on the design you created in Exercise 1a. Enter the program, saving it as **Home1.java**. Then execute the program. Follow your instructor's requirement for submitting output. Save your source code and your .class file in the Chap03 folder of your Student Disk.

   (Windows users can copy the active window or dialog box by pressing Alt+Print Scrn to copy the active window or dialog box to the Clipboard. Each time a new dialog box appears during execution, you can save the output to a separate document using a program such as Microsoft Word. If this is done, name your document **Home1Screens.doc** then print the Home1Screens document and attach it to a printed copy of your program.)

   (Unix users should save their .class file to disk, then either submit the disk or send the file electronically to their instructor.)

   Following are copies of dialog boxes that should appear as your program executes. The exact appearance depends on the data entered.

   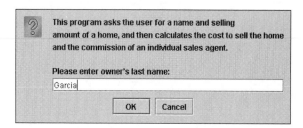

   Figure 3-1 Enter owner's name dialog box

   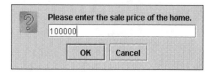

   Figure 3-2 Enter the sale price of the home dialog box

   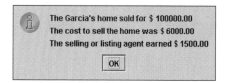

   Figure 3-3 Garcia's Home Sale dialog box

2. a. Redesign the program **Home1.java** in the Chap03 folder of your Student Disk. Change your input to read both input values into a String variable input stream. Tokenize the string to assign the name to a String variable and the amount to a double variable. Format the output of your decimal numbers to display two decimal places except when the decimal values are zero.

   Write your design in the following space. Your design should be a list of Java comments without any code.

2. b.   Write a Java program based on the design you created in Exercise 2a. Enter the program, saving it as **Home2.java**. Then execute the program. Follow your instructor's requirement for submitting output. Save your source code and your .class file in the Chap03 folder of your Student Disk.

(Windows users can select, copy, and paste text output into a block comment at the end of their program. Unix users should save their .class file to disk, then either submit the disk or send the file electronically to their instructor.)

Your instructor may prefer that you submit the .class file electronically with your program. Save your source code and your .class file in the Chap03 folder of your Student Disk.

Following is a copy of screen results that might appear depending on the data entered. The input entered by the user appears in bold.

```
This program asks the user for a name and selling
amount of a home, and then calculates the cost to sell the home
and the commission of an individual sales agent.

Please enter owner's last name and the sales price of the home:
Garcia 100000
The Garcia's home sold for $100000
The cost to sell the home was $6000
The selling or listing agent earned $1500
```

3. a.   Redesign the program **Home2.java** in the Chap03 folder of your Student Disk. Change your input to read both input values into a String variable input stream from a dialog box. Tokenize the string to assign the name to a String variable and the amount to a double variable.

Write your design in the following space. Your design should be a list of Java comments without any code.

3. b. Write a Java program based on the design you created in Exercise 3a. Enter the program, saving it as **Home3.java**. Then execute the program. Follow your instructor's requirement for submitting output. Save your source code and your .class file in the Chap03 folder of your Student Disk.

(Windows users can copy the active window or dialog box by pressing Alt+Print Scrn to copy the active window or dialog box to the Clipboard. Each time a new dialog box appears during execution, you can save the output to a separate document using a program such as Microsoft Word. If this is done, name your document **Home3Screens.doc** then print the Home3Screens document and attach it to a printed copy of your program.)

(Unix users should save their .class file to disk, then either submit the disk or send the file electronically to their instructor.)

Following are copies of dialog boxes that should appear as your program executes. The exact appearance depends on the data entered.

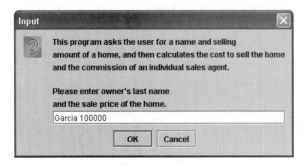

Figure 3-4   Enter owner's last name and sale price of the home dialog box

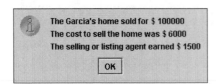

Figure 3-5   Home sale calculations dialog box

LAB 3.4 USING FILES FOR INPUT AND OUTPUT

Inputting data from the keyboard and displaying the output to the screen is convenient when you are working with a small amount of data. For large amounts of data, this method is inefficient. Additionally, you might want to check input for accuracy before processing it, and save output for later uses. Data can be read from and written to a data file. A file is an area in secondary storage used to hold information. To input data from a file, you use the class FileReader, and to send output to a file, you use the classes FileWriter and PrintWriter. Both of these classes are contained in the package java.io and require the import statement. Additionally, you must declare and associate appropriate class variables with the input/output sources.

The class FileReader contains the methods read and readLine. If you need to tokenize the data stored in the file, you can declare a StringTokenizer variable and initialize this variable using the object name.

To store output of a program in a file, you use the class FileWriter and associate it with the destination, the drive name and the filename. The class FileWriter contains the methods print, println, and flush. Output files must be closed using the method close once they are completed. This ensures that the output buffer is emptied. The class StringTokenizer does not have the method close. Therefore, you can only use the method close with the input file variable.

An input file must exist before it can be opened. If it does not exist, then the statement to associate the object with the input file fails and it throws a FileNotFoundException exception. An output file does not have to exist before it is opened. If it does exist, by default, the old contents are erased when the file is opened.

Objectives

In this lab, you use files for input and output.

After completing this lab, you will be able to:

- Associate file variables with I/O sources.
- Open and close input and output files.
- Read data from input files.
- Write data to output files.
- Work with multiple data files.

Estimated completion time: **50–60 minutes**

Using Files for Input and Output

Write complete Java programs from the instructions and output examples given.

1. a.   *Critical Thinking Exercise*: Design a Java program that a small gift shop could use to order merchandise. The wholesaler requires that you send your order as a file over a modem. Create your order file by entering your input through dialog boxes and writing to an output file. The order information for each item consists of two lines. The first line contains the quantity of an item, a blank, the wholesale cost for all items, and an end of line character. The second line contains the description of the item and an end of line character. Design your program to ask for two different items to order. Create a file named **order.out** with the following information:

   4   12.84   Wine Stoppers
   2   35.64   Silver Cheese Trays

   Write your design in the following space. Your design should be a list of Java comments without any code.

1. b. Write a Java program based on the design you created in Exercise 1a. Enter the program, saving it as **Gifts1.java**. Then execute the program. Follow your instructor's requirement for submitting output. Save your source code, your .class file, and your **order.out** file in the Chap03 folder of your Student Disk.

(Windows users can copy the active window or dialog box by pressing Alt+Print Scrn to copy the active window or dialog box to the Clipboard. Each time a new dialog box appears during execution, you can save the output to a separate document using a program such as a Microsoft Word. If this is done, name your document **Gifts1Screens.doc** then print the Gifts1Screens document and attach it to a printed copy of your program along with the printed copy of your **order.out** file.)

(Unix users should save their .class file to disk, then either submit the disk or send the file electronically to their instructor.)

Following are copies of dialog boxes that might appear depending on the data entered. After the dialog boxes, a copy of the order.out file that you created is displayed.

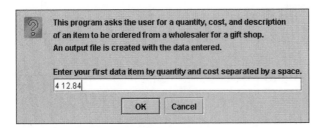

Figure 3-6   Program description dialog box

Figure 3-7   Enter description dialog box

Figure 3-8   Enter your second data item dialog box

Figure 3-9   Enter description dialog box with different input

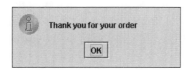

Figure 3-10   Thank you for your order dialog box

Order.out data file

```
4 12.84
Wine Stoppers
2 35.64
Silver Cheese Trays
```

2. a.   Design a program that builds on **Gifts1.java**. Copy the **order.out** file that you created in Lab 3.4 Exercise 1 and save it as **order.in** in the Chap03 folder on your Student Disk.

Once the gift shop has received an order from the wholesaler, the program should create an inventory file. Assume that all items ordered were received. Design your program to read the file **order.in** and write the file **inventory.out**. The file **inventory.out** will contain the number of items received, the retail cost that is found by dividing the wholesale cost by the quantity ordered and multiplying by 2.4, and the description of the item.

Write your design in the following space. Your design should be a list of Java comments without any code.

2. b. Write a Java program based on the design you created in Exercise 2a. Enter the program, saving it as **Gifts2.java**. Then execute the program. Follow your instructor's requirement for submitting output. Save your source code, your .class file, and your **inventory.out** file in the Chap03 folder of your Student Disk.

(Windows users can copy the active window or dialog box by pressing Alt+Print Scrn to copy the active window or dialog box to the Clipboard. Each time a new dialog box appears during execution, you can save the output to a separate document using a program such as Microsoft Word. If this is done, name your document **Gifts2Screens.doc** then print the Gifts2Screens document and attach it to a printed copy of your program along with the printed copy of your **inventory.out** file.)

(Unix users should save their .class file to disk, then either submit the disk or send the file electronically to their instructor.)

Following are copies of dialog boxes that might appear depending on the data entered when the order.out and order.in files were created. After the dialog boxes is a copy of the inventory.out file.

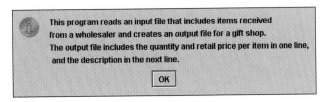

Figure 3-11   Inventory program description dialog box

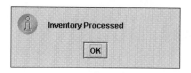

Figure 3-12   Inventory Processed dialog box

Inventory.out data file

```
4 7.70
Wine Stopper
2 42.77
Silver Cheese Tray
```

CONTROL STRUCTURES 1 (SELECTION)

In this chapter, you will:

♦ Learn about control structures

♦ Examine relational and logical operators

♦ Explore how to form and evaluate logical (Boolean) expressions

♦ Discover how to use the selection control structures if, if…else, and switch in a program

CHAPTER 4: ASSIGNMENT COVER SHEET

Name _____   Date _____

Section _____

Lab Assignments	Grade
Lab 4.1 Using Relational and Logical Operators to Evaluate Logical (Boolean) Expressions	
Lab 4.2 Using the Selection Control Structures if and if…else	
Lab 4.3 Using Nested if and if…else Statements	
Lab 4.4 Using the Conditional Operator (?:)	
Lab 4.5 Using the switch Selection Control Structure (Critical Thinking Exercise)	
Total Grade	

See your instructor or the introduction to this book for instructions on submitting your assignments.

LAB 4.1 USING RELATIONAL AND LOGICAL OPERATORS TO EVALUATE LOGICAL (BOOLEAN) EXPRESSIONS

A conditional statement is a control structure that allows a program to execute a selection of alternative statements depending on whether the condition is true or false. The program evaluates a condition by comparing two operands. In Java, this condition is called a logical (Boolean) expression. The relational comparison is done through relational operators and applies to all primitive data types. It also uses the Unicode Collating Sequence. Unicode is the recognized standard used in Java for character formats and is a subset of the ASCII standard. Table 4-1 describes each operator.

Table 4-1 Java Operators

Operator	Description
==	equal to
!=	not equal to
<	less than
<=	less than or equal to
>	greater than
>=	greater than or equal to

The String class provides the compareTo() method to compare objects of the String type. The syntax to use this method is `str1.compareTo(str2)`. When you use this method, the program returns a negative value, zero, or a positive value, depending on the result of the comparison. For example: `str1.compareTo(str2)` returns the following:

- An integer value less than 0 if str1 is less than str2

- 0 if str1 is equal to str2

- An integer value greater than 0 if str1 is greater than str2

As a programmer, you use the binary logical (Boolean) operators && (and) along with || (or) to combine logical expressions. The unary logical (Boolean) operator ! (not) reverses the value of the logical expression. The && (and) operator evaluates to false unless both Boolean expressions are true. The || (or) operator evaluates to true unless both Boolean expressions are false.

Like mathematical expressions, relational expressions have an order of precedence for evaluation. Parentheses can override the precedence of operators. Table 4-2 lists the precedence of operators and the order of evaluation.

Table 4-2 Operator Precedence

Operators	Precedence	Evaluation
!, +, - (unary operators)	First	Right to left
*, /, %	Second	Left to right
+,-	Third	Left to right
<, <=, >=, >	Fourth	Left to right
==, !=	Fifth	Left to right
&&	Sixth	Left to right
||	Seventh	Left to right
= (assignment operator)	Last	Right to left

A compound expression is evaluated from left to right. As soon as the value of the entire logical expression is known, the evaluation stops. This is known as short-circuit evaluation.

Objectives

In this lab, you evaluate Boolean expressions using relational and Boolean operators. Additionally, you learn to evaluate these expressions by the order of precedence of their operators.

After completing this lab, you will be able to:

- Evaluate logical expressions formed by the relationship of two operands.
- Use relational operators to evaluate the three primitive data types double, char, and int.
- Use the compareTo method to compare String variables.
- Use logical (Boolean) operators to evaluate combined logical expressions.
- Evaluate logical (Boolean) expressions by the correct order of precedence.
- Recognize logical expressions that can be short-circuit evaluations.

Estimated completion time: **30–40 minutes**

Using Relational and Logical Operators to Evaluate Logical (Boolean) Expressions

Evaluate the logical (Boolean) expressions in the following exercises and circle the correct answer after your evaluation. For char and String types, use the Unicode collating sequence.

Expression	Result (Circle the correct answer)
1. int num1 = 3, num2 = 2; (num1 > num2)	T F
2. double hours = 12.8; (hours > 40.2)	T F
3. int funny = 7; (funny !=1)	T F
4. char letter = 'A'; ('a' < letter)	T F
5. int count = 1; count <= 4;	T F
6. double y = -2.3; y >= 0.0;	T F

Expression Use the following values: x = false, y = false, z = true	Result (Circle all possible answers)
1. ! (x || y) || z	T F short-circuit
2. x && z && y	T F short-circuit
3. ! x || (y || ! z)	T F short-circuit
4. x || (z && (y || x))	T F short-circuit
5. true || ! z && y	T F short-circuit
6. ! (x || y) || x	T F short-circuit
7. z && x && y	T F short-circuit
8. ! x || (y || ! z)	T F short-circuit
9. x || (y && (x || z))	T F short-circuit
10. false || ! x && y	T F short-circuit

Expression Use the following values: x = false, y = false, z = true	Result (Circle all possible answers)
1. String name1 = "Aaron"; String name2 = "aaron"; name1.compareTo(name2)	T F
2. String name1 = "Aaron"; String name2 = "Aardvark"; name1.compareTo(name2)	T F
3. Boolean flag = true; int a = 2, b = 5, c = 10; (a * b <= c && ! flag)	T F
4. String name1 = "Aaron"; String word = "A"; name1.compareTo(word)	T F

LAB 4.2 USING THE SELECTION CONTROL STRUCTURES IF AND IF...ELSE

Java uses logical expressions to implement the selection control structures. There are two selections, or branch control structures: if statements and the switch structure. A one-way selection uses the if statement, which uses the reserved word if followed by a logical (Boolean) expression. The two-way selection uses the if...else statement, which builds on the if statement by offering an alternative selection following the reserved word else.

Objectives

In this lab, you become acquainted with one-way selection, the if statement. The statement or block of statements following the keyword if are executed when the expression evaluates to true. If you need to use more than one statement, a block is required. You also become acquainted with two-way selection, the if...else statement.

After completing this lab, you will be able to:

- Work with one-way selection, which evaluates either to true or false and is followed either by single statements or multiple statements.

- Work with two-way selection, which evaluates either to true or false and is followed either by single statements or multiple statements.

Estimated completion time: **20-30 minutes**

Using the Selection Control Structure if

Indicate which of the following output statements Java would execute. To do so, step through the statements, and then write what should be displayed.

Use the following two assignment statements for Exercises 1 through 7 of this lab.

```
int x = 6;
boolean found = false;
```

1. if (x >10)
       System.out.println("x is greater than 10.\n");
   System.out.println("Selection allows decision making.\n");

2. if (x == 6)
       System.out.println("A match is found.\n");
   System.out.println("Sequence continues after selection is complete.\n");

3. if (x < 8)
   {
      System.out.println("x is within the range.\n");
      System.out.println("This is a true statement.\n");
   }
   System.out.println("And, after selection, the next statement is executed.\n");

4. if (x == 6 || found)
      System.out.println("Problem 4 is true.\n");
   System.out.println("End of Problem 4\n");

5. if (x == 6 && found)
      System.out.println("Problem 5 is true.\n");
   System.out.println("End of Problem 5\n");

6. if (x !=6 && !found)
      System.out.println("Problem 6 is true.\n");
   System.out.println("End of Problem 6\n");

7. if (x > 0 && x < 10)
      System.out.println("x is in range\n");
   System.out.println("The value of x is " + x + ".\n");

Use the following two assignment statements for Exercises 8 through 14 of this lab.

```
int x = 6;
boolean found = false;
```

8. if (x > 10)
        System.out.println("x is greater than 10.\n");
    else
        System.out.println("x is less than or equal to 10.\n");
    System.out.println("Selection allows decision making.\n");

9. if (x == 6)
        System.out.println("A match is found.\n");
    else
        System.out.println("A match was not found.\n");
    System.out.println("Sequence continues after selection is complete.\n");

10.   if (!(x < 8))
        {
            System.out.println("x is within the range.\n");
            System.out.println("This is a true statement.\n");
        }
    else
        {
            System.out.println("x is out of range.\n");
            System.out.println("This is a false statement.\n");
        }
    System.out.println("After selection, the next statement is executed.\n");

11. if (x >= 5)
        {
        }
    else
        System.out.println("Have a good day.\n");
    System.out.println("The value of x is " + x + '\n');

```
12. if (x == 6 && found)
        System.out.println( "Problem 5 is true.\n");
    else
    {
        System.out.println( "Problem 5 is false.\n");
        System.out.println( "Both conditions must be true.\n");
    }
    System.out.println("End of Problem 5\n");
```

```
13. if (x !=6 && !found)
        System.out.println( "Problem 6 is true.\n");
    else
        System.out.println( "Problem 6 is false.\n");
    System.out.println( "End of Problem 6\n");
```

```
14. if (x > 0 && x < 10)
        System.out.println( "x is in  range\n");
    else
        System.out.println( "x is not in range\n");
```

LAB 4.3 USING NESTED IF AND IF...ELSE STATEMENTS

The statement(s) executed in a selection can be any valid Java statement. This includes an if statement located within another if or if...else statement. These statements are called nested statements. When the selection requires more than one alternative, use the nested if statement.

An else statement is not required; however, when used, all else statements must be paired with an if. In a nested if statement, Java associates an else with the most recent incomplete if—that is, the most recent if that has not been paired with an else.

An alternative to writing nested if...else statements is to write compound Boolean expressions.

Objectives

In this lab, you evaluate Boolean expressions in nested if statements.

After completing this lab, you will be able to:

- Match the else statement with the appropriate if statement.

- Know when to nest and when not to nest if statements.

- Write code using nested ifs.

- Write compound Boolean expressions using if...else statements.

Estimated completion time: **40–50 minutes**

Using Nested if and if...else Statements

Indicate which of the following output statements Java would execute. To do so, step through the statements, and then write what should be displayed.

1. int temperature = 78;
   int month = 6;
   String name = "Pat Boone";
   if (temperature >= 70 && month >=6)
       System.out.println("Wear sandals\n");
   else if (name == "Pat Boone")
       System.out.println("Wear white shoes\n");
   else
       System.out.println("Wear black shoes\n");

2. a. What is the output of the program when temperature = 70, month = 5, and name = "Pat Boone"?

2. b.   What is the output of the program when temperature = 60, month = 5, and name = "Pat Boone"?

2. c.   What is the output of the program when temperature = 60, month = 5, and name = "Your name"?

3. a.   Design a Java program that asks the user for three names. Using compound and nested if statements, display the names in alphabetical order. Write your design in the following space. Your design should be a list of Java comments without any code.

Following are copies of dialog boxes that should appear after running the program one time.

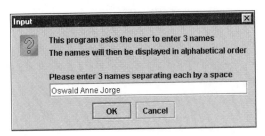

Figure 4-1   Enter three names dialog box for first test

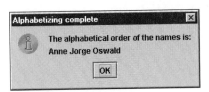

Figure 4-2   Alphabetizing complete dialog box for first test

3. b. Write a Java program based on the design you created in Exercise 3a. Enter the program, saving it as **NameSort.java** in the Chap04 folder on your Student Disk. Then execute the program four times, entering the names in a different order each time.

- Enter the names Oswald, Anne, and Jorge separated by spaces with no commas.

- Enter the names Oswald, Jorge, and Anne separated by spaces with no commas.

- Enter the names Anne, Oswald, and Jorge separated by spaces with no commas.

- Enter the names Jorge, Anne, and Oswald separated by spaces with no commas.

As your program executes, print the screen each time a new dialog box appears and paste the output in a document, such as a Microsoft Word or WordPad document. (In Windows, press Alt+Print Scrn to copy the active window or dialog box to the Clipboard. Then open a document and press Ctrl+V to paste the screen.) Name your document **NameSortScreens.doc**. Print the NameSortScreens document and attach it to a printed copy of your program. Save your source code and screen document in the Chap04 folder of your Student Disk.

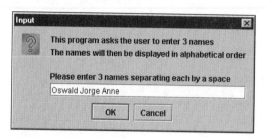

Figure 4-3   Enter three names dialog box for second test

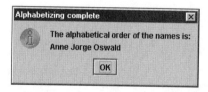

Figure 4-4   Alphabetizing complete dialog box for second test

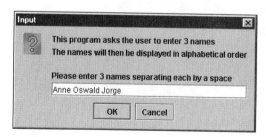

Figure 4-5   Enter three names dialog box for third test

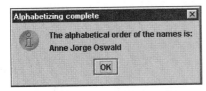

Figure 4-6   Alphabetizing complete dialog box for third test

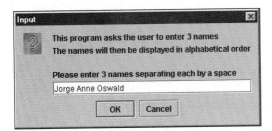

Figure 4-7   Enter three names dialog box for fourth test

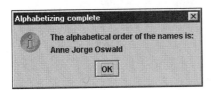

Figure 4-8   Alphabetizing complete dialog box for fourth test

LAB 4.4 USING THE CONDITIONAL OPERATOR (?:)

You can write certain if...else statements concisely by using the conditional operator in Java. The conditional operator, written as ?:, is a ternary operator, which means that it takes three arguments. The general syntax for the conditional operator (?:) follows:

(expression1) ? expression2 : expression 3;

For example, examine the following code.

```
int x = 10, sum = 0;
if(x == 10)
    sum = x + 3;
else
    sum = x - 3;
```

You can write these statements using the conditional operator:

```
int x = 10, sum = 0;
(x==10) ? sum = x + 3 : sum = x - 3;
```

In the previous examples, sum would be assigned 13 since x is equal to 10.

Notice that this code does not use the reserved word if or a semi-colon (;) after the true statement.

The conditional expression is evaluated as follows: If expression1 evaluates to true, the result of the conditional expression is expression2. Otherwise, the result of the conditional expression is expression3.

Objectives

In this lab, you rewrite if...else statements using the conditional operators (?:).

After completing this lab, you will be able to:

- Write if...else statements using the conditional operators (?:).

Estimated completion time: **10–15 minutes**

Using the Conditional Operator (?:)

Rewrite the following if...else statements using the conditional operator (?:). Assume the declaration statement:

1. double value = 8.9;
   if (value > 10.6)
       System.out.println("x is greater than 10.\n");
   else
       System.out.println("x is less than or equal to 10.\n");

2. int x = 4;
       if (x == 6)
           System.out.println("A match is found.\n");
       else
           System.out.println("A match was not found.\n");

LAB 4.5 USING THE SWITCH SELECTION CONTROL STRUCTURE

The third control structure, called the switch statement, gives the program the power to choose from among many alternatives.

A switch structure evaluates an expression, then uses the value of the expression to perform the actions specified in the statements that follow the reserved word `case`. The value of the expression must be integral and is sometimes called the selector. An integral value is a value that evaluates to an integer value.

The syntax of the switch statement is as follows:

```
    switch (expression)
{
case value1:  statements1
            break;
case value2:  statements2
            break;
        ...
case valuen:  statementsn
            break;
default: statements
}
```

The switch statement executes according to the following rules:

- When the value of the expression matches a case value, the statements execute until either a break statement is found or the end of the switch structure is reached.

- If the value of the expression does not match a case value, the statements following the default label execute. If there is no match and no default label, the entire switch statement is skipped.

The switch statement is an elegant way to implement multiple selections. If multiple selections involve a range of values, you should convert each range to a finite set of values. For instance, if all values 60 to 69 are the range of values, you could divide by 10, and then use the 6 as the finite value.

Objectives

In this lab, you convert a nested if...else statement to a switch statement.

After completing this lab, you will be able to:

- Write switch control statements using the break statement.

- Write switch control statements using the fall-through capability.

Estimated completion time: **30–40 minutes**

Using the Selection switch Control Structure

Write programs that use the switch statement, and then test them with different values.

1. a.   *Critical Thinking Exercise*: Design a Java program that uses the switch statement and asks the user to select one of three television models. The program should provide a description of the models. Using the switch statement fall-through capability, display the model chosen, the description, and the price. The user should make a selection by model number:

   - Model 100 comes with remote control, timer, and stereo sound and costs $1000.

   - Model 200 comes with all features of model 100, plus picture-in-picture; it costs $1200.

   - Model 300 comes with all features of model 200 plus HDTV, flat screen, and 16 × 9 aspect ratio; it costs $2400.

   Write your design in the following space. Your design should be a list of Java comments without any code.

1. b. Write a Java program based on the design you created in Exercise 1a. Enter the program, saving it as **TVmodel.java** in the Chap04 folder on your Student Disk. Execute the program three times, selecting a different model with each execution. As your program executes, print the screen each time a new dialog box appears and paste the output in a document, such as a Microsoft Word or WordPad document. (In Windows, press Alt+Print Scrn to copy the active window or dialog box to the Clipboard. Then open a document and press **Ctrl+V** to paste the screen.) Name your document **TVmodelScreens.doc**. Print the TVmodelScreens document and attach it to a printed copy of your program. Save your source code and screen document in the Chap04 folder of your Student Disk.

Following are copies of dialog boxes that should appear.

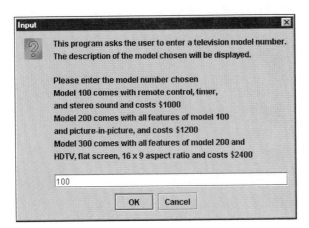

Figure 4-9   Selecting a television model dialog box for first test

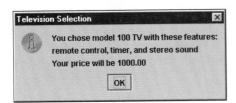

Figure 4-10   Television Selection dialog box for first test

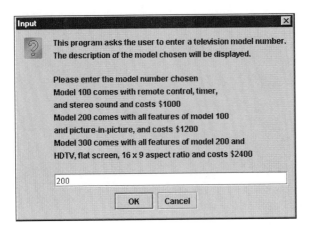

Figure 4-11   Selecting a television model dialog box for second test

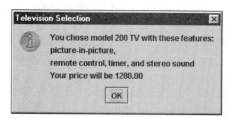

Figure 4-12 Television Selection dialog box for second test

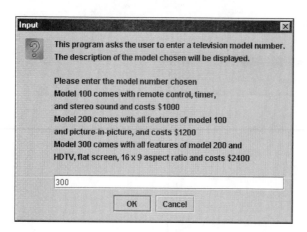

Figure 4-13 Selecting a television model dialog box for third test

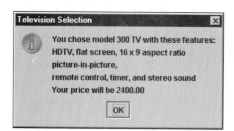

Figure 4-14 Television Selection dialog box for third test

Critical
Thinking

2. a. *Critical Thinking Exercise*: Design a program for a builder that allows the user to select floor options for building a home. The program should use an input dialog box to explain the purpose and use of the program, list flooring options, and ask the user to select one of the options by a numeric value. Use the switch statement. Display an information dialog box to display the selection made, the description, and the price. Use the following descriptions for the program:

```
This program asks the user to enter a choice
of flooring for a new home.
Enter the number that matches your flooring choice
1: Scored concrete, costs $3000
2: Carpeting comes with a $5000 allowance
3: Wood floors in the living area,
carpeting in the bedrooms, tile in the bath areas,
and a $5000 carpet allowance, totaling $10,000
```

Write your design in the following space. Your design should be a list of Java comments without any code.

2. b.   Write a Java program based on the design you created in Exercise 2a. Enter the program, saving it as **Flooring.java** in the Chap04 folder on your Student Disk. Then execute the program three times, selecting a different model with each execution. As your program executes, print the screen each time a new dialog box appears and paste the output in a document, such as a Microsoft Word or WordPad document. (In Windows, press Alt+Print Scrn to copy the active window or dialog box to the Clipboard. Then open a document and press **Ctrl+V** to paste the screen.) Name your document **FlooringScreens.doc**. Print the FlooringScreens document and attach it to a printed copy of your program. Save your source code and screen document in the Chap04 folder of your Student Disk.

Following are copies of dialog boxes that should appear.

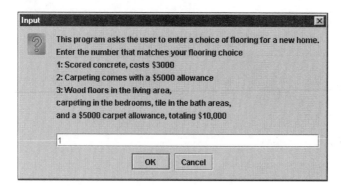

Figure 4-15   Select flooring dialog box for first test

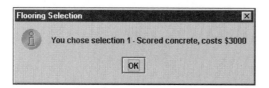

Figure 4-16   Flooring Selection dialog box for first test

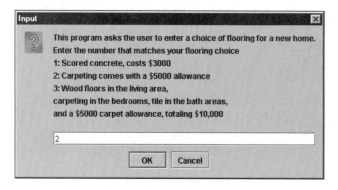

Figure 4-17   Select flooring dialog box for second test

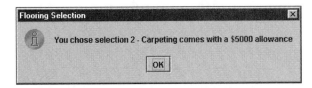

Figure 4-18   Flooring Selection dialog box for second test

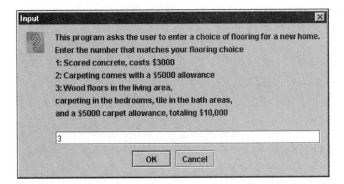

Figure 4-19   Select flooring dialog box for third test

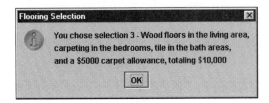

Figure 4-20   Flooring Selection dialog box for third test

5

CONTROL STRUCTURES II
(REPETITION)

In this chapter, you will:

♦ Learn about repetition (looping) control structures

♦ Explore how to construct and use count-controlled, sentinel-controlled, flag-controlled, and EOF-controlled repetition structures

♦ Examine break and continue statements

♦ Discover how to form and use nested control structures

Chapter 5: Assignment Cover Sheet

Name _____   Date _____

Section _____

Lab Assignments	Grade
Lab 5.1 Using the while Looping (Repetition) Structure	
Lab 5.2 Using the for Looping (Repetition) Structure	
Lab 5.3 Using the do...while Looping Repetition Structure (Critical Thinking Exercise)	
Lab 5.4 Using break and continue Statements	
Lab 5.5 Using Nested Control Structures (Critical Thinking Exercise)	
Total Grade	

See your instructor or the introduction to this book for instructions on submitting your assignments.

LAB 5.1 USING THE WHILE LOOPING (REPETITION) STRUCTURE

The three looping (repetition) structures, while, for, and do...while are reserved words in Java and used when you want a program to repeat a set of statements. The three different types of looping structures offer flexibility in coding. This lab focuses on the while loop.

The reserved word while acts on a Boolean expression, which serves as a decision-maker. Rarely, the expression accomplishes the entire work of the loop. This lab will not cover that situation. Generally, the work of the loop is accomplished within the body of the loop, which can include one or more statements, and is executed when the expression evaluates to true. The expression is reevaluated after each iteration of the statements until the expression evaluates to false. An exit condition must exist within a loop; otherwise, an infinite loop will occur.

A looping expression contains the loop control variable. The variable must be initialized before it is evaluated and updated within the body of the loop to provide an exit condition. All loops with loop control variables require the following:

1. An initialization of the loop control variable.

2. Evaluation of the loop condition. If the loop condition is false, the body of the loop never executes. If true, the body of the loop is executed.

3. An update of the loop control variable.

4. Repetition of steps 2 and 3 until the loop condition evaluates to false.

There are four types of while loops: counter-controlled, sentinel-controlled, flag-controlled, and EOF (end of file) controlled.

Objectives

In this lab, you become acquainted with all four types of while loops.

After completing this lab, you will be able to:

- Write a counter-controlled while loop when you know exactly how many pieces of data need to be read.

- Write a sentinel-controlled while loop that uses a special sentinel value to end the loop.

- Write a flag-controlled while loop that uses a Boolean variable as a decision-maker, and evaluates to false to end the loop.

- Write an EOF-controlled while loop that continues until the program reaches the end of the file.

Estimated completion time: **50–60 minutes**

Using the while Looping (Repetition) Structure

Design and write code for the Java programs that use while loops.

1. a. Design a Java program that asks for the number of students registered in a course. The user should be prompted to enter the number of students enrolled in a course. If the number of students is greater than 0, use a counter-controlled while loop to prompt the user to enter the names of the students registered for the class. Create an output file that contains the names of the students in the class. Display a message to the user when the program is complete.

Following is a copy of the screen results that might appear after running your program, depending on the data entered. The input entered by the user is in bold.

```
This program asks the user to enter the number and names of students in a
course.

How many students are registered for this class? 10

Enter the student's name: George Smith

Enter the student's name: Elaine Sanders

Enter the student's name: Jack Cunningham

Enter the student's name: Susie Brown

Enter the student's name: Marvella Garcia

Enter the student's name: Tony Peterson

Enter the student's name: John Jones

Enter the student's name: Mary Evans

Enter the student's name: Nancy Drew

Enter the student's name: Lola Zapata

The class is full.
```

Write your design in the following space. Your design should be a list describing what happens at each line in the program, or should use the format your instructor requires.

1. b. Write a Java program based on the design you created in Exercise 1a. Enter your program and name it **Roster1.java**. Name your output file **student1.dat**.

Step through your code by hand and complete a memory chart showing what occurs in memory when the Java code is executed.

To fill out the memory table, use multiple lines for each variable, if necessary. On one line, enter declaration information. Write the name of the declared variable, its data type, and the line number at declaration. On the next line in the memory table, enter initialization information for that variable. Enter the value in memory of the initialized variable and the line number of the initialization. For a variable that changes more than once in the loop, enter the line numbers where the variable changes.

Your answers will vary. The following memory chart shows an example of how a chart might start.

Variable name	Data type	Value in memory	Line number at declaration	Line number when initialized	Line numbers when changed
limit	int	?	14	21	27

Execute your program. Then copy the output and save it in a block comment at the end of your program. Save your source code and output data file in the Chap05 folder of your Student Disk.

The output file should list student names. Print your output file and attach it to your work.

2. a. Design a program to simulate the order processing of a hardware store. To fill an order, workers place items on a conveyor belt to be grouped, billed, and shipped. Each item has a UPC code that designates the name of the item and its price. When an order is complete, a worker places a bar on the conveyor belt to separate the order from the next order. The bar has a UPC code of 999. The computer system scans the UPC code of each item and records its price. When the system reads the code on the bar, it creates a bill, which it writes to an output file for further processing later.

In programming, a specific value to designate the end of a loop is called a sentinel value. The UPC code of 999 is used as the sentinel value.

The output file contains the product name on one line followed by the price of each item on the next line. Prompt the user to scan the next item. When the system reads the value 999, display a message to the user indicating the number of items that have been scanned.

Following is a copy of the screen results that might appear after running your program, depending on the data entered. The input entered by the user is shown in bold.

```
This order-processing program simulates using a
code reader to scan an item and create an invoice.

Please scan the name of the first item: hammer
Please scan the price of the hammer: 9.95
Please scan the name of the next item: saw
Please scan the price of the saw: 20.15
Please scan the name of the next item: shovel
Please scan the price of the shovel: 35.40
Please scan the name of the next item: 999

All items scanned.
```

Write your design in the following space. Your design should be a list describing what happens at each line in the program, or should use the format your instructor requires.

2. b. Write a Java program based on the design you created in Exercise 2a. Enter your program and name it **Scan1.java**. Name your output file **invoice1.dat**.

After entering your code but before executing your program, step through your code by hand and complete a memory chart showing what occurs in memory when the Java code is executed.

To fill out the memory table, use multiple lines for each variable, if necessary. On one line, enter declaration information. Write the name of the declared variable, its data type, and the line number at declaration. On the next line in the memory table, enter initialization information for that variable. Enter the value in memory of the initialized variable and the line number of the initialization. For a variable that changes more than once in the loop, enter the line numbers where the variable changes.

Variable name	Data type	Value in memory	Line number at declaration	Line number when initialized	Line numbers when changed

Execute your program. Test your program with the following input:

```
hammer
9.95
saw
20.15
shovel
35.40
999
```

Copy the output and save it in a block comment at the end of your program. Save your source code and output data file in the Chap05 folder of your Student Disk. Print your output file and attach to your work.

3. a. The file **invoice1.dat** created in Exercise 2 consists of a list of items with a description on one line followed by the price of the item on the next line. Design a program that prompts the user to enter an item. The item entered will be used to search a list in the **invoice1.dat** file until the program finds the item in the list or the end of file is reached. If the item is found, display the name and price of the item. If the item is not found, display the message that the item was not in the list. Format the price to show two decimal places. Use a compound flag-controlled `while` loop containing the Boolean value found and the EOF control.

Figure 5-1 shows the screen results that might appear after running your program, depending on the data entered.

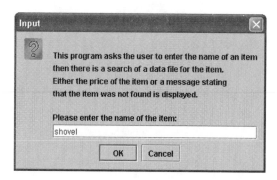

Figure 5-1   Input dialog box for first order processing program

Depending on the string entered and the data in the file, the output would resemble Figure 5-2.

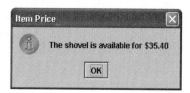

Figure 5-2   Item Price dialog box for first order processing program

Write your design in the following space. Your design should be a list that describes what happens at each line in the program, or should use the format your instructor requires.

3. b. Write a Java program based on the design that you created in Exercise 3a. After entering your code but before executing your program, step through your code by hand and complete a memory chart showing what occurs in memory when the Java code is executed.

To fill out the memory table, use multiple lines for each variable, if necessary. On one line, enter declaration information. Write the name of the declared variable, its data type, and the line number at declaration. On the next line in the memory table, enter initialization information for that variable. Enter the value in memory of the initialized variable and the line number of the initialization. For a variable that changes more than once in the loop, enter the line numbers where the variable changes.

Variable name	Data type	Value in memory	Line number at declaration	Line number when initialized	Line numbers when changed

Save the program as **Find1.java** in the Chap05 folder on your Student Disk, and then compile, run, and test the program. Either copy the dialog boxes that appear and paste them into a document or print screens of the dialog boxes.

Test your program with the file **invoice1.dat** and with the following input:

```
shovel
```

Print your input file and program and attach them to your printed output screens to submit with your work.

4. a.   Consider the data file you created and processed in Exercises 2 and 3. Design a program that will read all of the data from the file **invoice1.dat** and total the price of all of the items. Because all data is read from a file, there are no prompts or input from the user. Display your data in currency format.

Depending on the information in the file, the output should resemble Figure 5-3.

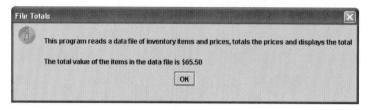

Figure 5-3   File Totals dialog box

Write your design in the following space. Your design should be a list describing what happens at each line in the program, or should use the format your instructor requires.

4. b. Write a Java program based on the design that you created in Exercise 4a.

After entering your code but before executing your program, step through your code by hand and complete a memory chart showing what occurs in memory when the Java code is executed.

To fill out the memory table, use multiple lines for each variable, if necessary. On one line, enter declaration information. Write the name of the declared variable, its data type, and the line number at declaration. On the next line in the memory table, enter initialization information for that variable. Enter the value in memory of the initialized variable and the line number of the initialization. For a variable that changes more than once in the loop, enter the line numbers where the variable changes.

Variable name	Data type	Value in memory	Line number at declaration	Line number when initialized	Line numbers when changed

Save the program as **Order1.java** in the Chap05 folder on your Student Disk, and then compile, run, and test the program. Test your program with the file **invoice1.dat**. Either copy the dialog boxes that appear and paste them into a document or print screens of the dialog boxes.

Print your input file and program and attach them to your printed output screens to submit with your work.

LAB 5.2 USING THE FOR LOOPING (REPETITION) STRUCTURE

The `for` looping structure, sometimes called a counted or indexed `for` loop, is a specialized form of the `while` loop that you use to simplify writing count-controlled loops.

To use the `for` looping structure, you write a `for` statement, where `for` is followed by the initialize statement, loop condition, and update statement enclosed within parentheses. The program executes a `for` loop in the following sequence:

1. The initialize statement executes.

2. The loop condition is evaluated. If the loop condition is false, the body of the loop never executes. If true, the body of the loop is executed.

3. The update statement executes after the body of the loop ends.

4. Steps 2 and 3 are repeated until the loop condition evaluates to false.

Objectives

In this lab, create programs that use the `for` loop.

After completing this lab, you will be able to:

- Write a `for` loop with an increment update condition.

- Write a `for` loop with a decrement update condition.

Estimated completion time: **50–60 minutes**

Using the for Looping (Repetition) Structure

Design and write programs using `for` loops.

1. a. Design a program that uses a `for` loop to calculate the factorial value entered by a user. A factorial number is a number multiplied by every factor between 1 and the number, inclusive. For instance, 3 factorial is 3 * 2 * 1. The user should be prompted to enter the factorial number. Display the result of the calculation. If a negative number is entered, display a message that only positive numbers will be calculated.

   Hint: It is not necessary to multiply by 1. If you test for the value of 1, you can initialize your loop counter to 2. Test your loop counter to be less than or equal to the number entered. Increment your loop counter. Initialize your answer to 1. Multiply your answer by your counter in each iteration of the loop.

   Following is a copy of the screen results that might appear after running your program, depending on the data entered. The input entered by the user is shown in bold.

   ```
   This program asks the user for a positive integer number,
   computes the factorial value, and displays the answer.
   Please enter a positive number: 5
   The factorial of 5 is 120
   ```

   Write your design in the following space. Your design should be a list describing what happens at each line in the program, or should use the format your instructor requires.

1. b.   Write a Java program based on the design that you created in Exercise 1a. After entering your code but before executing your program, step through your code by hand and complete a memory chart showing what occurs in memory when the Java code is executed.

To fill out the memory table, use multiple lines for each variable, if necessary. On one line, enter declaration information. Write the name of the declared variable, its data type, and the line number at declaration. On the next line in the memory table, enter initialization information for that variable. Enter the value in memory of the initialized variable and the line number of the initialization. For a variable that changes more than once in the loop, enter the line numbers where the variable changes.

Variable name	Data type	Value in memory	Line number at declaration	Line number when initialized	Line numbers when changed

Save the program as **CalcFac1.java** in the Chap05 folder on your Student Disk, and then compile, run, and test the program. Test your program with the following input:

5

Copy the instructions, input, and output that are displayed, and paste them in a block comment at the end of your program. Then print your program to submit with your work.

2. a.   Redesign Exercise 1 to calculate a factorial number using a `for` loop, setting the loop counter to the factorial value input by the user. Then decrement your counter.

Following is a copy of the screen results that might appear after running your program, depending on the data entered. The input entered by the user is shown in bold.

```
This program asks the user for a positive integer number,
computes the factorial value, and displays the answer.
Please enter a positive number: 5
The factorial of 5 is 120
```

Write your design in the following space. Your design should be a list describing what happens at each line in the program, or should use the format your instructor requires.

2. b. Write a Java program based on the design that you created in Exercise 2a. After entering your code but before executing your program, step through your code by hand and complete a memory chart showing what occurs in memory when the Java code is executed.

To fill out the memory table, use multiple lines for each variable, if necessary. On one line, enter declaration information. Write the name of the declared variable, its data type, and the line number at declaration. On the next line in the memory table, enter initialization information for that variable. Enter the value in memory of the initialized variable and the line number of the initialization. For a variable that changes more than once in the loop, enter the line numbers where the variable changes.

Variable name	Data type	Value in memory	Line number at declaration	Line number when initialized	Line numbers when changed

Save the program as **CalcFac2.java** in the Chap05 folder on your Student Disk, and then compile, run, and test the program. Test your program with the following input:

5

Copy the instructions, input, and output that are displayed, and then paste them in a block comment at the end of your program. Then print your program to submit with your work.

LAB 5.3 USING THE DO...WHILE LOOPING REPETITION STRUCTURE

The third repetition structure is the do...while loop. The do...while loop differs from both the while loop and the for loop. The while loop is called a pre-test loop because the loop condition is evaluated before the loop begins. In both the while loop and for loop, the body of the loop may be skipped depending on the result of the condition.

The do...while loop is a post-test loop. This means that the loop condition is tested at the end of the loop body; therefore, the do...while loop will always be executed at least once.

Objectives

In this lab, you create programs that use the do...while loop.

After completing this lab, you will be able to:

■ Write a do...while counter-controlled loop when you know exactly how many pieces of data need to be read.

■ Write a do...while sentinel-controlled loop that uses a special sentinel value to end the loop.

■ Write a do...while flag-controlled loop that uses a Boolean variable as a decision-maker, and evaluates to false to end the loop.

■ Write a do...while EOF-controlled loop that continues until the program reaches the end of the file.

Estimated completion time: **20-30 minutes**

Using the do...while Looping Repetition Structure

Rewrite code for the programs you designed in Lab 5.1 using a do...while loop instead of a while loop.

1. a.   Redesign the program you created in Lab 5.1 Exercise 1 using a do...while loop. The user should be prompted to enter the number of students enrolled in a course. If the number of students is greater than 0, use a counter-controlled while loop to prompt the user to enter the names of the students registered for the class. Create an output file that contains the names of the students in the class. Display a message to the user when the program is complete.

Validate the input value to make sure it is greater than 0.

Following is a copy of the screen results that might appear after running your program, depending on the data entered. The input entered by the user is in bold.

```
This program asks the user to enter the number and names of students in
a course.

How many students are registered for this class? 10

Enter the student's name: George Smith

Enter the student's name: Elaine Sanders

Enter the student's name: Jack Cunningham

Enter the student's name: Susie Brown

Enter the student's name: Marvella Garcia
```

```
Enter the student's name: Tony Peterson

Enter the student's name: John Jones

Enter the student's name: Mary Evans

Enter the student's name: Nancy Drew

Enter the student's name: Lola Zapata

The class is full.
```

Write your design in the following space. Your design should be a list describing what happens at each line in the program, or should use the format your instructor requires.

1. b. Write a Java program based on the design you created in Exercise 1a. Enter your program and name it **Roster2.java**. Name your output file **student2.dat**.

Step through your code by hand and complete a memory chart showing what occurs in memory when the Java code is executed.

To fill out the memory table, use multiple lines for each variable, if necessary. On one line, enter declaration information. Write the name of the declared variable, its data type, and the line number at declaration. On the next line in the memory table, enter initialization information for that variable. Enter the value in memory of the initialized variable and the line number of the initialization. For a variable that changes more than once in the loop, enter the line numbers where the variable changes.

Variable name	Data type	Value in memory	Line number at declaration	Line number when initialized	Line numbers when changed

Execute your program. Then copy the output and save it in a block comment at the end of your program. Save your source code and output data file in the Chap05 folder of your Student Disk.

2. a. Redesign the program you created in Lab 5.1 Exercise 2 that creates an invoice using a do...while loop. You will write a record for the item named 999. When an order is completed, a bar with a UPC code of 999 is placed on the conveyor belt and is also scanned. When the bar is scanned, each item is scanned and an invoice is created. The invoice is written to an output file for further processing later. Recall that the UPC code of 999 is used as the sentinel value. The output file contains the product name on one line followed by the price of each item on the next line. Prompt the user to scan the next item. Display a message and then the number of items that have been scanned when the value 999 is read.

Following is a copy of the screen results that might appear after running your program, depending on the data entered. The input entered by the user is shown in bold.

```
This order-processing program simulates using a
code reader to scan an item and create an invoice.

Please scan the name of the first item: hammer
Please scan the price of the hammer: 9.95
Please scan the name of the next item: saw
Please scan the price of the saw: 20.15
Please scan the name of the next item: shovel
Please scan the price of the shovel: 35.40
Please scan the name of the next item: 999

All items scanned.
```

Write your design in the following space. Your design should be a list describing what happens at each line in the program, or should use the format your instructor requires.

2. b.   Write a Java program based on the design you created in Exercise 1a. Enter your program and name it **Scan2.java**. Name your output file **invoice2.dat**.

Step through your code by hand and complete a memory chart showing what occurs in memory when the Java code is executed.

To fill out the memory table, use multiple lines for each variable, if necessary. On one line, enter declaration information. Write the name of the declared variable, its data type, and the line number at declaration. On the next line in the memory table, enter initialization information for that variable. Enter the value in memory of the initialized variable and the line number of the initialization. For a variable that changes more than once in the loop, enter the line numbers where the variable changes.

Variable name	Data type	Value in memory	Line number at declaration	Line number when initialized	Line numbers when changed

Execute your program. Test your program with the following input:

```
hammer
9.95
saw
20.15
shovel
35.40
999
```

Copy the output and save it in a block comment at the end of your program. Save your source code and output data file in the Chap05 folder of your Student Disk. Print your output file and attach to your work.

3. a.   *Critical Thinking Exercise*: Redesign the program you created in Lab 5.1 Exercise 3 that creates an invoice to be a compound flag-controlled do...while loop. The expression should evaluate to true until either a Boolean value named found is set or the EOF occurs. The file **invoice2.dat** created in Exercise 2 lists descriptions of items on one line followed by the price of the item on the next line. Design a program that prompts the user to enter an item. The item entered will be used to search a list in the **invoice2.dat** file until the program finds the item in the list or the end of file is reached. If the item is found, display the name and price of the item. If the item is not found, display the price or the message that the item was not in the list. Format the price to show two decimal places.

Figure 5-4 shows the screen results that might appear after running your program, depending on the data entered.

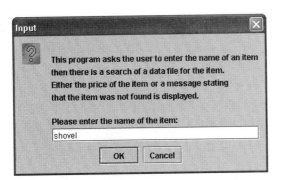

Figure 5-4   Input dialog box for search program

Depending on the string entered and the data in the file, the output would resemble Figure 5-5.

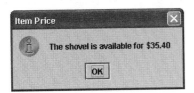

Figure 5-5   Item Price dialog box for search program

Write your design in the following space. Your design should be a list describing what happens at each line in the program, or should use the format your instructor requires.

3. b.   Write a Java program based on the design that you created in Exercise 3a. After entering your code but before executing your program, step through your code by hand and complete a memory chart showing what occurs in memory when the Java code is executed.

To fill out the memory table, use multiple lines for each variable, if necessary. On one line, enter declaration information. Write the name of the declared variable, its data type, and the line number at declaration. On the next line in the memory table, enter initialization information for that variable. Enter the value in memory of the initialized variable and the line number of the initialization. For a variable that changes more than once in the loop, enter the line numbers where the variable changes.

Variable name	Data type	Value in memory	Line number at declaration	Line number when initialized	Line numbers when changed

Save the program as **Find2.java** in the Chap05 folder on your Student Disk, and then compile, run, and test the program. Either copy the dialog boxes that appear and paste them into a document or print screens of the dialog boxes.

Test your program with the file **invoice2.dat** and with the following input:

shovel

Print your input file and program and attach them to your printed output screens to submit with your work.

4. a.   Redesign the program you created in Lab 5.1 Exercise 4 that considers the data file you created and processed in Exercises 2 and 3. Use a do...while loop instead of a while loop. Read all of the data from the file **invoice2.dat** and calculate the total price of all of the items. Because all data is read from a file, there are no prompts or input from the user. Display your data in currency format.

Depending on the information in the file, the output should resemble Figure 5-6.

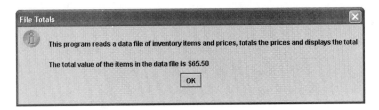

Figure 5-6   File Totals dialog box for second program

Write your design in the following space. Your design should be a list describing what happens at each line in the program, or should use the format your instructor requires.

4. b.   Write a Java program based on the design that you created in Exercise 4a.

After entering your code but before executing your program, step through your code by hand and complete a memory chart showing what occurs in memory when the Java code is executed.

To fill out the memory table, use multiple lines for each variable, if necessary. On one line, enter declaration information. Write the name of the declared variable, its data type, and the line number at declaration. On the next line in the memory table, enter initialization information for that variable. Enter the value in memory of the initialized variable and the line number of the initialization. For a variable that changes more than once in the loop, enter the line numbers where the variable changes.

Variable name	Data type	Value in memory	Line number at declaration	Line number when initialized	Line numbers when changed

Save the program as **Order2.java** in the Chap05 folder on your Student Disk, and then compile, run, and test the program. Test your program with the file **invoice2.dat**. Either copy the dialog boxes that appear and paste them into a document or print screens of the dialog boxes.

Print your input file and program and attach them to your printed output screens to submit with your work.

LAB 5.4 USING BREAK AND CONTINUE STATEMENTS

The break and continue statements alter the flow of control in a program. When you use a break in a switch statement or in a repetition structure, you provide an immediate exit from the structure. The program continues to execute with the first statement after the structure.

Use a continue statement in a repetition structure to end the current iteration only and proceed with the next iteration of the loop. In a `for` loop, the next statement is the update statement. Use a break statement in a repetition structure to end the entire repetition. Use these constructs sparingly. They are introduced for informational purposes, but are not suggested for general solutions.

Objectives

In this lab, you use break and continue statements to alter the control of a loop.

After completing this lab, you will be able to:

- Execute a loop until a break statement is encountered.

- Execute a loop and skip over the remaining loop statement when a continue statement is encountered and proceed in the loop until the loop terminates.

Estimated completion time: **20-30 minutes**

Using break and continue Statements

In the following exercises, you evaluate the output in repetition control structures that use the continue or break statements. You also write programs from designs that use the continue or break statements.

1. a. Design a program that uses a `for` loop to enter 20 numbers and add those that are positive. Use the continue statement if the number entered is not positive. This will result in only the positive numbers being summed and the negative numbers being ignored. The user is to be prompted to enter the numbers. Display the total.

    Following is a copy of the screen results that might appear after running your program, depending on the data entered. The input entered by the user is shown in bold.

    ```
    This program asks the user to enter 20 numbers,
    adds the positive numbers, and displays the totals.
    Please enter 20 numbers; separate each with a space:
    2 3 1 -6 10 2 6 5 9 -10 9 2 -4 3 1 2 -6 7 3 2
    The sum of the positive numbers is: 67
    ```

    Write your design in the following space. Your design should be a list describing what happens at each line in the program, or should use the format your instructor requires.

1. b.   Write a Java program based on the design you created in Exercise 1a. Enter your program and name it **Sum.java**. Step through your code by hand and complete a memory chart showing what occurs in memory when the Java code is executed.

To fill out the memory table, use multiple lines for each variable, if necessary. On one line, enter declaration information. Write the name of the declared variable, its data type, and the line number at declaration. On the next line in the memory table, enter initialization information for that variable. Enter the value in memory of the initialized variable and the line number of the initialization. For a variable that changes more than once in the loop, enter the line numbers where the variable changes.

Variable name	Data type	Value in memory	Line number at declaration	Line number when initialized	Line numbers when changed

Execute your program. Test your program with the following input:

```
2 3 1 -6 10 2 6 5 9 -10 9 2 -4 3 1 2 -6 7 3 2
```

Copy the instructions, input, and output that are displayed, and then paste them in a block comment at the end of your program. Save your source code and output data file in the Chap05 folder of your Student Disk. Print your program to submit with your work.

2. a.   Redesign the program that you created in Lab 5.4 Exercise 1 using a break statement instead of the continue statement. This will result in only the positive values being summed until the first negative value is encountered. Then the program should not consider any more values.

Following is a copy of the screen results that might appear after running your program, depending on the data entered. The input entered by the user is shown in bold.

```
This program asks the user to enter 20 numbers,
adds the positive numbers, and displays the totals.
Please enter 20 numbers; separate each with a space:
2 3 1 -6 10 2 6 5 9 -10 9 2 -4 3 1 2 -6 7 3 2
The sum of the numbers entered until a negative number is entered is: 6
```

Write your design in the following space. Your design should be a list describing what happens at each line in the program, or should use the format your instructor requires.

2. b. Write a Java program based on the design you created in Exercise 2a. Enter your program and name it **SumwBrk.java**. Step through your code by hand and complete a memory chart showing what occurs in memory when the Java code is executed.

To fill out the memory table, use multiple lines for each variable, if necessary. On one line, enter declaration information. Write the name of the declared variable, its data type, and the line number at declaration. On the next line in the memory table, enter initialization information for that variable. Enter the value in memory of the initialized variable and the line number of the initialization. For a variable that changes more than once in the loop, enter the line numbers where the variable changes.

Variable name	Data type	Value in memory	Line number at declaration	Line number when initialized	Line numbers when changed

Execute your program. Test your program with the following input:

```
2 3 1 -6 10 2 6 5 9 -10 9 2 -4 3 1 2 -6 7 3 2
```

Copy the instructions, input, and output that are displayed, and then paste them in a block comment at the end of your program. Save your source code and output data file in the Chap05 folder of your Student Disk. Print your program to submit with your work.

LAB 5.5 USING NESTED CONTROL STRUCTURES

One control structure can be nested (contained) within another control structure, and that structure can be nested within another control structure. The control structures do not have to be of the same type.

Inner control structures close before the outer control structure closes.

Objectives

In this lab, you use a nested control structure within a control structure.

After completing this lab, you will be able to:

■ Recognize the beginning and end of control structures.

■ When an inner control structure is a `for` loop, recognize that the loop is reinitialized with each iteration of an outer loop.

Estimated completion time: **40–50 minutes**

Using Nested Control Structures

In the following exercises, you design and write programs that use nested control structures.

1. a. Design a Java program that asks a user to enter a character and a sentence. The program counts the number of times the character entered appears in the sentence. Display a message that tells how often the specified character appears in the sentence.

   Figures 5-7 and 5-8 show the screen results that might appear after running your program, depending on the data entered.

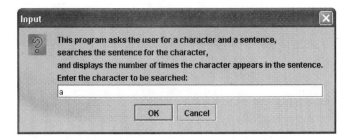

Figure 5-7 Input dialog box to enter character to find

Figure 5-8 Input dialog box to enter sentence to search

Depending on the string entered and the data in the file, the output would resemble Figure 5-9.

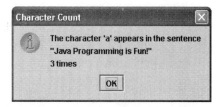

Figure 5-9   Character Count dialog box

Write your design in the following space. Your design should be a list describing what happens at each line in the program, or should use the format your instructor requires.

1. b.   Write a Java program based on the design you created in Exercise 1a. Enter your program and name it **ChCount1.java**. Step through your code by hand and complete a memory chart showing what occurs in memory when the Java code is executed.

   To fill out the memory table, use multiple lines for each variable, if necessary. On one line, enter declaration information. Write the name of the declared variable, its data type, and the line number at declaration. On the next line in the memory table, enter initialization information for that variable. Enter the value in memory of the initialized variable and the line number of the initialization. For a variable that changes more than once in the loop, enter the line numbers where the variable changes.

Variable name	Data type	Value in memory	Line number at declaration	Line number when initialized	Line numbers when changed

   Save **ChCount1.java** in the Chap05 folder on your Student Disk, and then compile, run, and test the program. Either copy the dialog boxes that appear and paste them into a document or print screens of the dialog boxes.

   Test your program with the following input:

   Character to enter: `'a'`

   Sentence to enter: `"Java Programming is Fun!"`

   Print your input file and program and attach them to your printed output screens to submit with your work.

2. a.   *Critical Thinking Exercise*: Redesign the program that you created in Lab 5.5 Exercise 1 to allow the user to enter additional sentences. Create an outer loop that asks the user if they would like to enter another sentence. The outer loop should continue as long as the user answers 'y'. Remember to reinitialize your character counter each time you go through your outer loop. You will need one more prompt to ask users if they want to enter another sentence.

   Figures 5-10 and 5-11 show the screen results that might appear after running your program, depending on the data entered.

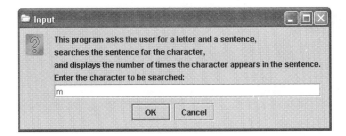

Figure 5-10   Entering the character to find

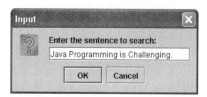

Figure 5-11   Entering the sentence to search

Depending on the string entered and the data in the file, the output would resemble Figures 5-12 through 5-16.

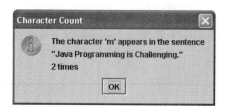

Figure 5-12   Character Count dialog box for second program

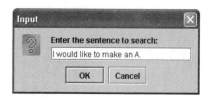

Figure 5-13   First Input dialog box

Figure 5-14   Second Input dialog box

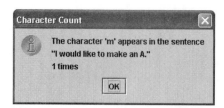

Figure 5-15   Results of second test

Figure 5-16   Third Input dialog box

Write your design in the following space. Your design should be a list describing what happens at each line in the program, or should use the format your instructor requires.

2. b.   Write a Java program based on the design you created in Exercise 2a. Enter your program and name it **ChCount2.java**. Step through your code by hand and complete a memory chart showing what occurs in memory when the Java code is executed.

To fill out the memory table, use multiple lines for each variable, if necessary. On one line, enter declaration information. Write the name of the declared variable, its data type, and the line number at declaration. On the next line in the memory table, enter initialization information for that variable. Enter the value in memory of the initialized variable and the line number of the initialization. For a variable that changes more than once in the loop, enter the line numbers where the variable changes.

Variable name	Data type	Value in memory	Line number at declaration	Line number when initialized	Line numbers when changed

Save **ChCount2.java** in the Chap05 folder on your Student Disk, and then compile, run, and test the program. Either copy the dialog boxes that appear and paste them into a document or print screens of the dialog boxes.

Test your program with the following input:

Character to enter: `'m'`

Sentence to enter: `"Java Programming is Challenging."`

Answer to enter: `yes`

Sentence to enter: `"I would like to make an A."`

Answer to enter: `no`

Print your input file and program and attach them to your printed output screens to submit with your work.

3. a.   *Critical Thinking Exercise*: Design a program that prints column titles and row titles in a spreadsheet format. The values 1, 2, 3, 4, 5 should appear in the first five columns of the first five rows. Use a for loop to output the column headings. Use nested **for** loops to output the row number and the values within the rows and columns. The output should look like the following.

```
     A     B     C     D     E
1    1     2     3     4     5
2    1     2     3     4     5
3    1     2     3     4     5
4    1     2     3     4     5
5    1     2     3     4     5
```

Write your design in the following space. Your design should be a list describing what happens at each line in the program, or should use the format your instructor requires.

3. b.   Write a Java program based on the design you created in Exercise 3a. Enter your program and name it **Table.java**. Step through your code by hand and complete a memory chart showing what occurs in memory when the Java code is executed.

To fill out the memory table, use multiple lines for each variable, if necessary. On one line, enter declaration information. Write the name of the declared variable, its data type, and the line number at declaration. On the next line in the memory table, enter initialization information for that variable. Enter the value in memory of the initialized variable and the line number of the initialization. For a variable that changes more than once in the loop, enter the line numbers where the variable changes.

Variable name	Data type	Value in memory	Line number at declaration	Line number when initialized	Line numbers when changed

Execute your program. Then copy the output and save it in a block comment at the end of your program. Save your source code and output data file in the Chap05 folder of your Student Disk.

CHAPTER

6

GRAPHIC USER INTERFACE (GUI) AND OBJECT ORIENTED DESIGN (OOD)

In this chapter, you will:

- Learn about basic GUI components
- Explore how the GUI components JFrame, JLabel, JTextField, and JButton work
- Become familiar with the concept of event-driven programming
- Discover events and event handlers
- Explore object-oriented design
- Learn about members of a class

CHAPTER 6: ASSIGNMENT COVER SHEET

Name _____   Date _____

Section _____

Lab Assignments	Grade
Lab 6.1 Extending the GUI component JFrame	
Lab 6.2 Accessing the Content Pane	
Lab 6.3 Using an Event Handler (Critical Thinking Exercise)	
Lab 6.4 Using Object-Oriented Design	
Lab 6.5 Implementing Classes and Operations (Critical Thinking Exercise)	
Total Grade	

See your instructor or the introduction to this book for instructions on submitting your assignments.

LAB 6.1 EXTENDING THE GUI COMPONENT JFRAME

The methods showInputDialog and showMessage produce dialog boxes to accept and display data. Those dialog boxes are displayed one at a time. An additional graphic user interface (GUI) tool allows a program to display the entire input and output simultaneously in an area called the window. The GUI components are placed in an area called the content pane of the window.

Every window has a title, width, and height. These window elements are called attributes. JFrame is a class that provides methods to control the attributes of a window. One way to create a window is to declare an object of the type JFrame and to use the following methods to manipulate the window:

- setSize() sets the width and height in pixels of the window

- setTitle() sets the titles of the window

- setVisible() displays the window

- setDefaultCloseOperation()closes the window

- addWindowListener() registers a window listener object to a JFrame

In addition to instantiating an object of the type JFrame to create a window, you can extend the definition of the class JFrame, or build "on top of" the class JFrame using inheritance. When using inheritance to create a window you need, you use a special type of method called a constructor in addition to the main method in the program. The constructor method has the same name as the name of the class. You create the new class by extending the existing class, JFrame, contained in the package javax.swing. Therefore, JFrame is the superclass of the class; and the class is known as the subclass of JFrame.

Objectives

In this lab, you design and write a program to extend the definition of the class JFrame.

After completing this lab, you will be able to:

- Create a window using JFrame.

- Write a constructor method for an application program PropertyTax1.

Estimated completion time: **15–20 minutes**

Extending the GUI Component JFrame

In the following exercises, you design and write a program that displays a window.

1. a. Design a program that extends the definition of the class JFrame to display a window on the screen. Name your class PropertyTax1, title your window "Calculation of Property Taxes," set the window's width to 400 pixels and height to 300 pixels, and terminate the program PropertyTax1 when the user closes the window.

Following is a copy of the screen results that might appear after running your program.

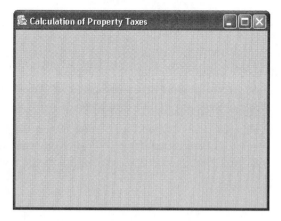

Figure 6-1   Calculation of Property Taxes window

Write your design in the following space. Your design should be a list describing what happens at each line in the program, or should use the format your instructor requires.

1. b. Write a Java program based on the design you created in Exercise 1a. Enter your program and name it **PropertyTax1.java**.

Save the program in the Chap06 folder on your Student Disk, and then compile, run, and test the program. Either copy the dialog box that appears and paste it into a document or print the screen of the dialog box.

LAB 6.2 ACCESSING THE CONTENT PANE

You use the method getContentPane() to access the content pane of the window. The components of the content pane are managed by a reference variable of the type Container to add GUI components to the content pane. You use the method add() to add an object to the pane, and the method setLayout() to set the layout of the pane. For instance, the setLayout() method allows you to arrange rows and columns in the pane. After the layout is set, you add components to the pane.

The class JLabel contains the constructor methods JLabel() to create a label with text, an icon, or both. The labels are set to be left-justified, right-justified, or centered in the field.

The class JTextField contains methods to manipulate the text fields of the content pane. You use the constructor method JTextField() to set the size of the text field, to initialize the object with the text specified, or to initialize the object with text specified and set the size of the text field. You use the method setText() to set the text field to the specified string. You use the method getText() to return the text contained in the text field. The method setEditable() controls whether text can be entered into the text field. You use the method addActionListener to register a listener object.

The class JButton contains methods to create buttons. You use the constructor method JButton() to initialize the button object with the icon specified, to initialize the button object to the text specified, or to initialize the button object to the text specified and the icon specified. You use the method setText() to set the text of the button to the specified string. You use the method getText() to return the text contained in a button, and the method setEditable() to set the button to accept or not accept text, but display results. Use the method addActionListener() to register a listener object for the button object.

Objectives

In this lab, you design and write a Java program to access the content pane using the classes JLabel, JTextField, and JButton.

After completing this lab, you will be able to:

- Access the content pane.
- Declare reference variables of the type Container, JLabel, JTextField, and JButton.
- Add objects to the content pane.
- Set the layout of the content pane.
- Create text labels.
- Create text fields.
- Create buttons.

Estimated completion time: **50–60 minutes**

Accessing the Content Pane

In the following exercises, you expand the program you designed and created in Lab 6.1.

1. a.   In this lab, you expand your **PropertyTax1.java** program that extends the definition of the class JFrame to display a window on the screen. You now design the code to allow access to the content pane.

   Design a Java program that creates the content pane to calculate property taxes. You need label fields and text fields to let users enter a home value, school tax rate, and county tax rate;

label fields and text fields to display the school tax, county tax, and total taxes; and buttons to calculate and exit the program. Additionally, set the layout of the content pane to create a grid of seven rows and two columns. You will not process any values yet.

Following is a copy of the screen results that might appear after running your program.

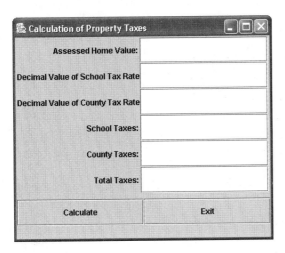

Figure 6-2 Calculation of Property Taxes window with content pane

Write your design in the following space. Your design should be a list describing what happens at each line in the program, or should use the format your instructor requires.

1. b. Write a Java program based on the design you created in Exercise 1a. Enter your program and name it **PropertyTax2.java**. Save the program in the Chap06 folder in your work folder.

LAB 6.3 USING AN EVENT HANDLER

An action event sends a message to another object known as an action listener. When the listener receives the message, it performs an action. For each JButton, you must specify the corresponding listener object; this is known as registering the listener. You must define the methods that are invoked when the event is sent to the listener.

The action event is handled by the class ActionListener—an interface—which contains the method actionPerformed(). You cannot instantiate an object of the type ActionListener. One way to register an action listener is to create a class on top of the method ActionPerformed. To build classes on top of interface classes, you use the modifier **implements**. You register the listener object (the handler) with the corresponding JButton.

Objectives

In this lab, you register an action listener by creating a class on top of the method ActionPerformed.

After completing this lab, you will be able to:

- Register an action listener to create a class on top of the method ActionPerformed.
- Use the modifier implements to build classes on top of classes.
- Create a listener object.
- Register the listener object (the handler) with the corresponding JButton.

Estimated completion time: **50–60 minutes**

Using an Event Handler

In the following exercises, you expand the program you designed and created in Lab 6.2.

1. a. *Critical Thinking Exercise*: This lab expands on your **PropertyTax2** program. Redesign your Java program to register private classes CalculateButtonHandler and ExitButtonHandler that implement the class ActionListener and a private class ExitButtonHandler. Associate the CalculateButtonHandler with the calculateB button and the ExitButtonHandler with the exitB button. Design code that calculates school taxes as the tax rate times the assessed value divided by 100. Display the decimal values of the tax rates with four decimal places, and the calculated taxes with two decimal places.

   Following is a copy of the screen results that might appear after running your program.

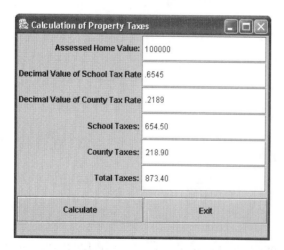

Figure 6-3   Calculation of Property Taxes window with results

Write your design in the following space. Your design should be a list describing what happens at each line in the program, or should use the format your instructor requires.

1. b.   Write a Java program based on the design you created in Exercise 1a. Enter your program and name it **PropertyTax3.java**. Save the program in the Chap06 folder in your work folder.

LAB 6.4 USING OBJECT-ORIENTED DESIGN

Object-oriented design (OOD) uses objects to design programs. To use an object, you do not need to know how the object is made. This information may be hidden from you. However, you need to know the functions of the object (such as buttons) and how to use them. You may use an object by itself or with other objects, but you cannot modify the functions of the object. To create objects you first need to learn to create classes; to know what type of classes to create, you need to know what an object stores and what operations are needed to manipulate an object's data.

The aim of OOD is to build software from software components called classes and to use the various methods provided by those classes. In OOD, you first identify the object, then identify the relevant data, and then identify operations needed to manipulate the object. One basic principle of OOD is encapsulation—the ability to combine data, and operations on that data, in a single unit.

OOD methodology can be expressed in the following steps:

1. Write a detailed description of the problem.

2. Identify all (relevant) nouns and verbs.

3. From the list of nouns, select objects. Identify data components of each object.

4. From the list of verbs, select the operations.

Objectives

In this lab, you read a problem and identify the components of the problem using the OOD methodology steps.

After completing this lab, you will be able to:

- Separate a problem statement into OOD methodology steps.

- Identify all nouns.

- Identify classes.

- Identify data members for each of the classes.

- Identify operations for each of the classes.

Estimated completion time: **20-30 minutes**

Using Object-Oriented Design

Consider the following problem:

Company XYZ needs a program to build a database concerning employee information. The program should do the following:

- Ask employees for their name and number of dependents claimed for tax purposes.

- Display a message to verify the number of tax deductions. (This will be one more than the number of dependents entered.)

- Let employees select whether they want personal health insurance or family health insurance.

- Display a message to verify the selection and tell each employee the cost of the selection.

- Let employees select whether they want to deduct union dues from their paycheck.

- Display a message to verify the selection and tell each employee the cost of the selection.

- Show the OOD solution of this problem.

Step 1: Identify all nouns.

Step 2: Identify class(es).

Step 3: Identify data members for each of the class(es).

Step 4: Identify operations for each of the objects (classes).

LAB 6.5 IMPLEMENTING CLASSES AND OPERATIONS

After you define relevant classes, data members, and relevant operations, the next step is to implement these in Java. To implement operations in Java, you write algorithms. Each algorithm is implemented with the help of Java's methods. Java provides the classes Integer, Double, Character, Long, and Float so that values of primitive data types can be treated as objects. These classes are called **wrappers**.

Included with this text are classes IntClass and DoubleClass, which are similar to the classes Integer and Double, respectively. They are found with your Chapter 7 student files. The constructor methods IntClass() are used to initialize the objects instantiated to 0. The method setNum() is used to set the data member to the parameter value. The method getNum() is used to retrieve a value. The method addToNum() is used to update the data value by the parameter value. The method compareTo() compares the data value with the parameter value. The method equals() compares the data value with the parameter value. The method toString() converts the value to a string.

Objectives

In this lab, you write a program based on the OOD design you developed in Lab 6.4 to create information for an employee database. Display a window with five rows and three columns.

After completing this lab, you will be able to:

- Implement a Java program from an OOD.

- Use the IntClass in a Java program.

Estimated completion time: **50–60 minutes**

Implementing Classes and Operations

In the following exercises, you write a program from an OOD design and use the user-defined IntClass.

Critical Thinking Exercise: Write a Java program based on the design you created in Lab 6.4. Enter your program and name it **EmployeeInfo.java**. Following is a copy of the screen results that might appear after running your program.

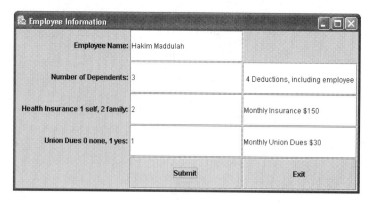

Figure 6-4   Employee Information window

Save the program in the Chap06 folder on your Student Disk, and then compile, run, and test the program. Either copy the dialog box that appears and paste it into a document or print the screen of the dialog box.

Test your program with the following input:

Employee Name: **Hakim Maddulah**

Number of Dependents: **3**

Health Insurance 1 self, 2 family: **2**

Union Dues 0 none, 1 yes: **1**

USER-DEFINED METHODS

In this chapter, you will:

♦ Learn about standard (predefined) methods and discover how to use them in a program

♦ Learn about user-defined methods

♦ Examine value-returning methods, including actual and formal parameters

♦ Explore how to construct and use a value-returning, user-defined method in a program

♦ Learn how to construct and use void methods in a program

♦ Explore variables as parameters

♦ Learn about the scope of an identifier

♦ Learn about method overloading

CHAPTER 7: ASSIGNMENT COVER SHEET

Name _____   Date _____

Section _____

Lab Assignments	Grade
Lab 7.1 Implementing Standard (Predefined) Methods	
Lab 7.2 Designing and Implementing a Program Using Standard (Predefined) Methods	
Lab 7.3 Implementing Value-Returning User-Defined Methods	
Lab 7.4 Designing and Implementing Value-Returning User-Defined Methods (Critical Thinking Exercise)	
Lab 7.5 Designing and Implementing Void User-Defined Methods with No Parameters and with Primitive Type Parameters (Critical Thinking Exercise)	
Lab 7.6 Designing and Implementing Void User-Defined Methods with Object Parameters	
Lab 7.7 Identifying the Scope of an Identifier	
Lab 7.8 Using Method Overloading	
Total Grade	

See your instructor or the introduction to this book for instructions on submitting your assignments.

LAB 7.1 IMPLEMENTING STANDARD (PREDEFINED) METHODS

A Java program is a collection of classes, and a class is a collection of methods and data members. Some methods are predefined, or standard methods, and are used to perform a particular task. Some predefined methods are mathematical methods. For example, sqrt(x) is a method in the class Math and is used to calculate the square root of a value. These methods are organized as a collection of classes, called class libraries.

The class Math contains predefined Java math methods and the class Character contains predefined character manipulations methods. To use predefined methods in a Java program, you must import the package containing the class.

Objectives

In this lab, you include the correct class library for standard methods, write method calls to standard methods, provide the missing code, and test the code. To complete this lab you need to use the toLowerCase, ceil, floor, and abs standard methods.

After completing this lab, you will be able to:

- Use standard (predefined) methods with parameters.

- Write method calls to standard (predefined) methods.

- Use values from value returning standard (predefined) methods.

Estimated completion time: **30–40 minutes**

Implementing Standard (Predefined) Methods

In this lab, you complete a Java program that uses the class Math.

1. Complete a program that asks the user to enter a floating-point number (either positive or negative). The program repeats while the user enters 'y' to continue. The program allows the user to enter either a lowercase or uppercase character. Use the ceil(), floor(), and abs() methods to determine the smallest whole number that is greater than or equal to the number entered, the largest whole number that is less than or equal to the number entered, and the absolute value of the number given. Use the toLowerCase() method to change a given character value to lowercase if the value is an uppercase value.

   Supply the missing code and import the correct package for the standard (predefined) methods used.

   Following is a copy of the screen results that might appear after running your program, depending on the data entered once all the changes have been made. The text entered by the user appears in bold.

   ```
   Enter a float number and I will tell you:
   the smallest whole number >= to the number,
   the largest whole number <= to the number,
   and the absolute value of the number.

   5.4

   The smallest whole number greater than 5.4 is 6.0
   The largest whole number less than 5.4 is 5.0
   The absolute value of 5.4 is 5.4

   Do you want to enter more data? y/n
   y
   ```

```
Enter a float number and I will tell you:
the smallest whole number >= to the number,
the largest whole number <= to the number,
and the absolute value of the number.

-8.8

The smallest whole number greater than -8.8 is -8.0
The largest whole number less than -8.8 is -9.0
The absolute value of -8.8 is 8.8


Do you want to enter more data? y/n
n
```

Complete the following Java program, replacing the bold comments with code as appropriate, and importing the package names where appropriate. Write appropriate method calls to a method defined in the class Math. For readability, leave the blank lines and comments that separate parts of the program. Save the program as **Numbersfixed.java** in the Chap07 folder on your Student Disk. Compile, execute, and test the program. After executing your program, select and copy everything that appears on your screen. Paste the copied text into a comment block at the end of your program.

```
/* include comments to identify the writer of the code and to describe
   the program */

import java.io.*;
import         // import the correct package for predefined Math methods

public class Numbers
{
public static void main(String[] args) throws IOException
{

        BufferedReader keyboard = new BufferedReader(
        new InputStreamReader(System.in));
        double x;
        String line;
        char again = 'y';

        while (again == 'y')
        { System.out.println("Enter a float number and I will tell "
            + "you:\n"
            + "the smallest whole number >= to the number,\n"
            + "the largest whole number <= to the number,\n"
            + "and the absolute value of the number.\n");

            x = Double.parseDouble(keyboard.readLine());

/*Include the code to import the class Math*/

        System.out.println("\nThe smallest whole number greater than "
            + x + " is " + /* smallest whole number >= to the number */
            + "\nThe largest whole number less than " + x + " is "
            + /* the largest whole number <= to the number */
            + "\nThe absolute value of " + x + " is "
            + /* the absolute value of the float number */ + "\n\n");

            System.out.println("Do you want to enter more data? y/n ");
            line = keyboard.readLine();
```

```
            again = line.charAt(0);
            again = /* the lowercase character entered by the user */ ;
        }

    }
}
```

LAB 7.2 DESIGNING AND IMPLEMENTING A PROGRAM USING STANDARD (PRE-DEFINED) METHODS

If a method returns a value, the method is described as being the data type of the return value. For instance, the pow method returns a double value, so pow is of type double. When using standard (pre-defined) methods, you only need to represent that method in the design with an explanation of the formal parameters required by the method and the return type.

Objectives

In this lab, you design and implement a Java program that uses standard (predefined) methods.

After completing this lab, you will be able to:

- Design and implement a program that uses standard (predefined) value-returning methods with parameters.

- Describe the use of each program module.

> Estimated completion time: **50–60 minutes**

Designing and Implementing a Program Using Standard (Predefined) Methods

In the following exercises, you answer questions to determine the design of a Java program. Each exercise can have several correct answers. The answers you choose will determine your program design.

1. Suppose a user wants to calculate the square of a number or the square root of a number, and display the results. To design this problem, what do you need to know about the standard methods that have this purpose?

2. The user will also enter a character value to designate which process is wanted. Should you make any assumptions about the case of the character entered? Would that require using any other standard method?

3. What variables do you need for user input and for calculations? What types are these variables?

4. The user should be allowed to continue processing until a value is entered to quit. What kind of loop works best in this situation?

5. Does the numeric value entered need any type of validation? Is that validation dependent on which math method is to be called?

6. What is the required data type and number of arguments required for the predefined methods you are using?

7. If the methods you are using are value returning, how will those returned values be handled?

8. Should your decimal numbers be formatted? If so, what class file is needed?

9. a. Design the program to calculate either the square of a number or the square root of a number and display the results.

Following is a copy of the screen results that might appear after running your program, depending on the data entered. The text entered by the user appears in bold.

```
Enter a float value: 6.2
Do you want the (s)quare or square (r)oot of 6.2: r
The square root of 6.2 is 2.4899799195977463

Do you want to enter more data? y/n: y
Enter a float value: -4.6
Do you want the (s)quare or square (r)oot of -4.6: r
You must have a positive number for square root.
Do you want the (s)quare or square (r)oot of -4.6: s
The number -4.6 squared has the value 21.159999999999997

Do you want to enter more data? y/n: y
Enter a float value: 3.9
Do you want the (s)quare or square (r)oot of 3.9: s
The number 3.9 squared has the value 15.209999999999999

Do you want to enter more data? y/n: y
Enter a float value: -4
Do you want the (s)quare or square (r)oot of -4.0: s
The number -4.0 squared has the value 16.0

Do you want to enter more data? y/n: n
```

Write your design in the following space. Your design should be a list describing what happens at each line in the program, or should use the format your instructor requires.

9. b.   Write a Java program based on the design you created in Exercise 9a. For readability, insert blank lines to separate parts of the program. Include comments to explain the different sections of code. Save the program as **SqrSqrt.java** in the Chap07 folder on your Student Disk. Compile, execute, and test the program. After executing your program, select and copy everything that appears on your screen. Paste the copied text into a comment block at the end of your program.

LAB 7.3 IMPLEMENTING VALUE-RETURNING USER-DEFINED METHODS IN A PROGRAM

Because Java does not provide every method you might ever need, you can write your own methods, called user-defined methods. User-defined methods can be value-returning methods or void methods.

You use, or call, a value-returning method in an expression. The expression can be part of an assignment statement or an output statement. A method call in a program causes the body of the called method to execute.

The visibility of the method determines where in a program the method can be used (called). Some of the modifiers are public, private, protected, static, abstract, and final. When more than one modifier is used, separate the modifiers with spaces. The following list defines the visibility of the methods used in this chapter. More information on modifiers will be introduced with classes. You can select one modifier among public, protected, and private. This lab focuses on public and private modifiers, as described in the following list:

- *public*—specifies that the method can be called outside the class

- *private*—specifies that the method cannot be called outside the class

A value-returning method returns a value via the return statement. The data type of the value returned is specified as the return type.

Objectives

In this lab, you complete a program that contains two value-returning user-defined methods.

After completing this lab, you will be able to:

- Write calls to value-returning user-defined methods with and without parameters.

- Write value-returning user-defined methods with and without parameters.

Estimated completion time: **30–40 minutes**

Implementing Value-Returning User-Defined Methods in a Program

In the following exercises, you examine Java programs that call value-returning user-defined methods. Value-returning methods can have formal parameters or no parameters.

1. The following program design contains two methods that have a string argument that will be used in the methods as a prompt to the user. The method getValue returns an integer value and the method getLetter returns a character.

    Provide the missing code designated by the comments. Your code should include calls to methods getValue and getLetter and headings to those methods. The program asks the user for today's year and month, and his or her year and month of birth. The program calculates and displays the user's age and continues when the user enters 'y'.

    Following is a copy of the screen results that might appear after running your program, depending on the data entered. The input entered by the user is in bold.

    ```
    This program asks you to enter today's year in 4 digits.
    Then it asks you to enter today's month number.

    In the next step you will be asked to enter the 4-digit year of your birth.
    ```

Then you will be asked to enter the month number of your birth.

The program will calculate and display how old you are in years and months.

```
Enter today's 4-digit year: 2005
Enter today's month number: 10
Enter the 4-digit year of your birth: 1986
Enter the month number of your birth: 8
You are 19 years and 2 months old.
```

Do you want to enter more data? y/n **n**

Complete the following Java program, replacing the bold comments with code as appropriate. For readability, insert blank lines to separate parts of the program. Include comments to explain the different sections of code. Save the program as **CalcAge.java** in the Chap07 folder on your Student Disk. Compile, execute, and test the program. After executing your program, select and copy everything that appears on your screen. Paste the copied text into a comment block at the end of your program.

```java
/* Write comments for programmer identification and to describe
   what the program does */

import java.io.*;
import java.lang.Math;

public class CalcAge
{
  static BufferedReader keyboard = new BufferedReader(
        new InputStreamReader(System.in));
  public static void main(String[] args) throws IOException
  {
      int currentYear = 0, currentMonth = 0, year, month, age;
      String line;
      char again = 'y';

      System.out.println("This program asks you to enter today's "
          + "year in 4 digits.\n"
          + "Then it asks you to enter today's month number.\n\n"
          + "In the next step you will be asked to enter the 4-digit "
          + "year of your birth.\n"
          + "Then you will be asked to enter the month number of your "
          + "birth.\n\n"
          + "The program will calculate and display how old you are "
          + "in years and months.\n\n");

      while (currentYear < 2002 || currentMonth < 1 ||
         currentMonth > 12)
      {
         currentYear = /* call the method getValue with the string
           argument "Enter today's 4-digit year: " */

         if (currentYear < 2002)
            System.out.println("You did not enter current year.\n");
         else
         {
            currentMonth = /* call the method getValue with the string
              argument "Enter today's month number: " */

            if (currentMonth < 1 || currentMonth > 12)
```

```
                        System.out.println("You did not enter a month between 1 "
                          + "and 12.\n");
                }
        }

        while (again == 'y')
        {
            year = /* call the method getValue with the string argument
                "Enter the 4-digit year of your birth: " */

            if (year > currentYear || year < 1)
            {
                System.out.println("You did not enter a valid year.\n");
                continue;
            }
            month = /* call the method getValue with the string argument
                    "Enter the month number of your birth " */

            if (month < 1 || month > 12)
            {
                System.out.println("You did not enter a valid month.\n");
                continue;
            }
            if (currentMonth > month)
            {
                age = currentYear - year;
                month = currentMonth - month;
            }

            else if (currentMonth == month)
            {
                age = currentYear - year;
                month = 0;
            }

            else    //currentMonth < month
            {
                age = currentYear - year - 1;
                month = 12 - month + currentMonth;
            }

            if ( (age < 0 || age > 120) || (age == 0 && month < 0) )
            {
                System.out.println("You did not enter valid dates.\n");
                continue;
            }
              System.out.println("You are " + age + " years and " + month
                    + " months old.\n");

            again = /* call the method getLetter with the string argument
                    "Do you want to enter more data? y/n " */

        } // end while
    } //end of main

/* Write the value-returning method heading for the method getValue
   that has a string formal parameter named message.
   (remember to code for IOExceptions) */


    {
```

```
            int value;
            System.out.print(message);
            System.out.flush();
            value = Integer.parseInt(keyboard.readLine());;
            return value;
        } //end of getValue

   /* Write the value-returning method heading for the method getLetter
      that has a string formal parameter named message.
      (remember to code for IOExceptions) */
        {
            char letter;
            String line;
            System.out.print(message);
            System.out.flush();
            line = keyboard.readLine();
            letter = line.charAt(0);
            return letter;
        } //end of getLetter

} //end of class
```

LAB 7.4 DESIGNING AND IMPLEMENTING VALUE-RETURNING USER-DEFINED METHODS IN A PROGRAM

One technique of designing a Java program is to break the design into modules. Each module designates a different step of the program. This allows you to focus on one part of the program at a time. The process of constructing, debugging, and perfecting part of a program one module at a time is called stepwise refinement.

Objectives

In this lab, you design the program using design modules.

After completing this lab, you will be able to:

■ Write a design for a program with user defined value-returning methods with and without formal parameters.

Estimated completion time: **40–50 minutes**

Designing and Implementing Value-Returning User-Defined Methods in a Program

In the following exercises, you design and write Java programs that use value-returning user-defined methods.

1. a. *Critical Thinking Exercise*: Design a program that asks the user to enter a year and then determines if it is a leap year. Be sure to tell the user what the program does. Your program should have a loop and continue when the user enters the character 'y'.

   Write three methods according to the following descriptions:

   ■ getYear has no formal parameters, asks the user to enter a year, and returns an integer value that is assigned to the integer variable year.

   ■ isLeap has an integer formal parameter, year, determines if the year is a leap year, and returns the Boolean value true if the year is a leap year and false if it is not. A year is a leap year if it is divisible by 4, but is not divisible by 100 except when divisible by 400. (The year 2000 was a leap year.)

   ■ moreData has a string formal parameter, asks the user to enter a 'y' or 'n' if they want to process another year, and returns a Boolean value that is assigned to the Boolean variable again.

   Be sure to include comments and display the results to the user.

   Following is a copy of the screen results that might appear after running your program, depending on the data entered. The input entered by the user is in bold.

```
This program asks you to enter a year in 4 digits.
The output will indicate whether the year you entered is a leap year.

Enter a year: 2003
2003 is not a leap year.

Do you want to enter more data? y/n: y
Enter a year: 2000
2000 is a leap year.

Do you want to enter more data? y/n: y
Enter a year: 1900
```

```
1900 is not a leap year.

Do you want to enter more data? y/n: y
Enter a year: 1800
1800 is not a leap year.

Do you want to enter more data? y/n: y
Enter a year: 2004
2004 is a leap year.

Do you want to enter more data? y/n: n
```

Write your design in the following space. Your design should be a list describing what happens at each line in the program, or should use the format your instructor requires.

1. b.   Write a Java program based on the design you created in Exercise 1a. Save the program as **LeapYear.java**, and then compile, run, and test the program. Copy the instructions, input, and output that are displayed, and then paste them in a block comment at the end of your program.

LAB 7.5 DESIGNING AND IMPLEMENTING VOID USER-DEFINED METHODS WITH PRIMITIVE TYPE PARAMETERS

The order that methods appear in a program does not matter because the main method is always executed first. Void methods are not called as part of an expression; the call is a stand-alone statement. A void method does not have a data type and does not need a return statement. You can use the keyword return with no value to exit the method or the method will exit at the end of the method definition. Void methods are useful for displaying information about the program or printing statements.

Objectives

In this lab, you write two void methods with no parameters.

After completing this lab, you will be able to:

- Use stepwise refinement as a program design technique.

- Call a void method with no parameters from the main method.

- Write a void method definition that has no parameters.

- Call a void method with parameters from the main method.

- Write a void method definition with parameters

Estimated completion time: **50–60 minutes**

Designing and Implementing Void User-Defined Methods with No Parameters and with Primitive Type Parameters

In the following exercises, you design and write Java programs that use void user-defined methods.

1. a. Design a program that displays instructions for using the program and displays a title for a Payroll Report. Design two void methods with no parameters, instructions, and reportTitle. The program will eventually process a payroll; however, in this exercise, you are only designing a driver (main), a method instructions to tell the user how to use the payroll program, and a method reportTitle to display the headings of the report that will be written later.

Your instructions method should output the following message:

```
                Instructions for Payroll Report Program
This program calculates a paycheck for each employee.
A text file will be created outside of the program with the following
information:
name, rate of pay, number of hours worked, and tax percentage to be
deducted.
The program will create a report in columnar format showing the
employee name, hourly rate, number of hours worked, tax rate, gross
pay, and net pay.

After all employees are processed, totals will be displayed, including
total gross amount and total net pay.
```

Your reportTitle method should output the following:

```
                Payroll Report
Employee        Hourly    Hours    Tax      Gross     Net
Name            Rate      Worked   Rate     Amount    Amount
```

Java does not require that you include method definitions in a particular order, but it is standard to put main before other method definitions. Be sure to include comments and display the results to the user.

Write your design in the following space. Your design should be a list describing what happens at each line in the program, or should use the format your instructor requires.

1. b. Write a Java program based on the design you created in Exercise 1a. Save the program as **Payroll1.java**, and then compile, run, and test the program. Copy the instructions, input and output that are displayed, and then paste them in a block comment at the end of your program.

2. a. *Critical Thinking Exercise*: This lab expands on your Payroll1 program, which gives instructions for using a payroll processing program, and provides report titles for a report. You now create a method with parameters of the primitive type that will, after processing, report the payroll values processed. You will not actually be processing any values at this time. You are only writing the methods that will write values formatted to two decimal positions when the methods are called.

In the main method, declare a string variable for employeeName and double variables for hourlyRate, hoursWorked, taxRate, grossAmount, and netAmount. Because you have not written the program-processing code yet, initialize all double values to 0.0 and string values to " ". Write a definition for a void method printEmployeeInfo with parameters for employeeName, hourlyRate, hoursWorked, taxRate, grossAmount, and netAmount. After the call to the reportTitle method, write a call to the printEmployeeInfo method. Output your report in columnar format. Allow 20 spaces for the name and 10 spaces for all other fields. Write a String method addBlanks to format a value to 10 spaces.

You may use the following design for your addBlanks method.

- Declare a string value initialized to a null string that will contain the number of spaces to write as separators for the report columns.

- Write a for loop that starts with the value 100000 minus the integer representation of the number that you are evaluating for adding blanks.

- Continue your loop as long as your number is positive.

- Update your loop counter by dividing the number by 10 each loop iteration.

- Concatenate a blank character to your line with each loop iteration.

- After your loop is complete, if your amount is less than 10, concatenate another blank character.

- If your amount is greater than 999, you must decrease your line by one blank character. (Use your substring method and your length method to decrease the line by one blank character.)

- Include a return line.

Your printEmployeeInfo method should output the following:

```
            0.00       0.00       0.00       0.00       0.00
```

Be sure to include comments and display the results to the user.

Write your design in the following space. Your design should be a list of what happens at each line in the program, or should use the format your instructor requires.

2. b. Write a Java program based on the design you created in Exercise 2a. Save the program as
Payroll2.java, and then compile, run, and test the program. Copy the instructions, input and
output that are displayed, and paste them in a block comment at the end of your program.

LAB 7.6 DESIGNING AND IMPLEMENTING VOID USER-DEFINED METHODS WITH OBJECT PARAMETERS

A formal parameter of the primitive type receives a copy of the actual parameter from the method call. However, a formal parameter that is a reference variable receives the location (memory address) of the corresponding actual parameter. You use reference parameters to share results with the calling method. Think of a reference parameter name as a "synonym" for the actual parameter name—representing the same memory location.

To pass strings as parameters to a method and change the actual parameter, you can use the class StringBuffer. The methods for string manipulation, append, and delete are contained in the class StringBuffer. However, you cannot use the assignment operator for StringBuffer variables.

Objectives

In this lab, you write a void method with reference parameters. Using stepwise refinement, you continue to build on the payroll program. You also create a text file of data to use in payroll processing.

After completing this lab, you will be able to:

- Call a void method with reference parameters from the main method.

- Write a void method definition with reference parameters.

Estimated completion time: **50–60 minutes**

Designing and Implementing Void User-Defined Methods with Object Parameters

In the following exercises, you design and write Java programs that use void user-defined methods with object parameters.

1. Create a text file to contain the data to process. You can use any text editor to create the file, but be sure to save in a text format. Use the following data and create a text file called **payroll.dat**:

John Smith

9.45 40 15

Jane Doe

12.50 45 15

Harry Morgan

20.00 40 20

Carmen Martinez

25.00 35 25

Jacintha Washington

50.85 60 35

2. a.   Continue your program design for your payroll program. Add a design for a Boolean method inputData with reference parameters to input an employee name, hourly rate, hours worked, and tax rate from the **payroll.dat** file. After the call to the reportTitle method, include a loop to allow for multiple data processing until all data has been read and processed. You must change your string variable employeeName to use the class StringBuffer instead of the class String. You must also change your double variables hourlyRate, hoursWorked, and taxRate to be reference variables of the class DoubleClass found in the Chapter 7 files of the textbook and import jpfpatpd.ch07.primitiveTypeClasses.DoubleClass. Now that you are processing data, you may need to make minor modifications to your printEmployeeInfo and reportTitle functions.

Following is a copy of the screen results that should appear after running your program.

```
                Instructions for Payroll Report Program
This program calculates a paycheck for each employee.
A text file will be created outside of the program with the following
information:
name, rate of pay, number of hours worked, and tax percentage to be
deducted.

The program will create a report in columnar format showing the
employee name, hourly rate, number of hours worked, tax rate, gross
pay, and net pay.

After all employees are processed, totals will be displayed, including
total gross amount and total net pay.
```

	Payroll Report				
Employee Name	Hourly Rate	Hours Worked	Tax Rate	Gross Amount	Net Amount
John Smith	9.45	40.00	15.00	0.00	0.00
Jane Doe	12.50	40.00	15.00	0.00	0.00
Harry Morgan	20.00	40.00	20.00	0.00	0.00
Carmen Martinez	25.00	35.00	25.00	0.00	0.00
Jacintha Washington	50.85	60.00	35.00	0.00	0.00

Write your design in the following space. Your design should be a list describing what happens at each line in the program, or should use the format your instructor requires.

2. b. Write a Java program based on the design you created in Exercise 2a. Save the program as **Payroll3.java**, and then compile, run, and test the program. Copy the instructions, input, and output that are displayed, and paste them in a block comment at the end of your program.

LAB 7.7 IDENTIFYING THE SCOPE OF AN IDENTIFIER

The scope of an identifier refers to where an identifier is accessible in the program. In a class, a variable or an object is accessible throughout the class, with the exception that a static method cannot access a nonstatic variable or object. An identifier declared within a block is accessible only within the block from the point at which it is declared until the end of the block. When a block is nested within another block, an identifier from the outer block is recognized in the inner block. The exception to this occurs if the inner block has an identifier of the same name.

The scope rule for the variable declared in a for statement is limited to only the body of the for loop.

Objectives

In this lab, you learn to recognize the difference between local and global variables and the scope of their identifiers.

After completing this lab, you will be able to:

- Use value parameters and reference variables in the same method.

Estimated completion time: **50–60 minutes**

Identifying the Scope of an Identifier

In the following exercises, you design and write methods for the payroll program.

1. a.   In this lab, you continue the stepwise refinement of the payroll program. In the payroll program, design new methods processPay and totalAmounts. Now all variables hourlyRate, hoursWorked, taxRate, grossAmount, and netAmount are to be declared as reference variables of the DoubleClass. However, you will use value parameters and reference variables when passing values to the processPay method. You may need to change your call to printEmployeeInfo. The void method totalAmounts uses the class double, and variables totalGrossAmount and totalNetAmount that have been declared before main.

   You calculate the grossAmount by multiplying the hoursWorked by the hourlyRate. All hours worked above 40 hours should be calculated at a time and a half rate. To find the netAmount, multiply the grossAmount by the taxRate divided by 100, and then subtract that amount from the grossAmount.

   You may need to adjust the spacing of your reportTitle and printEmployeeInfo functions.

   Be sure to include comments and display the results to the user.

Following is a copy of the screen results that might appear after running your program.

```
                Instructions for Payroll Report Program
This program calculates a paycheck for each employee.
A text file will be created outside of the program with the following
information:
name, rate of pay, number of hours worked, and tax percentage to be
deducted.

The program will create a report in columnar format showing the
employee name, hourly rate, number of hours worked, tax rate, gross
pay, and net pay.

After all employees are processed, totals will be displayed, including
total gross amount and total net pay.
```

```
                    Payroll Report
Employee                Hourly    Hours      Tax      Gross      Net
Name                    Rate      Worked     Rate     Amount     Amount

John Smith              9.45      40.00      15.00    378.00     321.30

Jane Doe                12.50     45.00      15.00    843.75     717.19

Harry Morgan            20.00     40.00      20.00    800.00     640.00

Carmen Martinez         25.00     35.00      25.00    875.00     656.25

Jacintha Washington     50.85     60.00      35.00    4576.50    2974.72
Totals                                                7513.25    5343.46
```

Write your design in the following space. Your design should be a list of what happens at each line in the program, or should use the format your instructor requires.

1. b. Write a Java program based on the design you created in Exercise 1a. Save the program as **Payroll4.java**, and then compile, run, and test the program. Copy the instructions, input, and output that are displayed, and paste them in a block comment at the end of your program.

LAB 7.8 USING METHOD OVERLOADING

In a Java program, methods can have the same name, but they must have a different set of parameters. The types of parameters in the method call determine which method to execute. This is called method overloading. The return type or void is not considered a part of method overloading.

Objectives

In this lab, you use method overloading according to the type of data being processed.

After completing this lab, you will be able to:

- Write methods of the same name with different formal parameter lists.

- Understand method overloading.

Estimated completion time: **30–40 minutes**

Using Method Overloading

In the following exercises, you design and write Java programs that use method overloading.

1. a. Design a program with multiple method definitions called dataOut, with each one having different value parameters listed in different orders. Call each dataOut method using a different list of parameters each time. Declare four variables:

   - A character letter assigned the value 'a'

   - A String name assigned the value "Hello"

   - An integer number assigned the value 5

   - A double value assigned the value 6.25

   Call dataOut with the following parameter lists:

   - char, String, int, double

   - String, int, double, char

   - int, double

   - char, String

   - char, int

   Be sure to include comments and display the results to the user.

Following is a copy of the screen results that might appear after running your program.

```
You called dataOut with the character a,
the string Hello,
the integer number 5,
and the double number 6.25.


You called dataOut with the string Hello,
the integer number 5,
the double number 6.25,
and the character a.


You called dataOut with the integer number 5
and the double number 6.25.


You called dataOut with the character a
and the string Hello.


You called dataOut with the character a
and the integer number 5.
```

Write your design in the following space. Your design should be a list describing what happens at each line in the program, or should use the format your instructor requires.

1. b. Write a Java program based on the design you created in Exercise 1a. Save the program as **PrintData.java**, and then compile, run, and test the program. Copy the instructions and output that are displayed, and paste them in a block comment at the end of your program.

CLASSES AND DATA ABSTRACTION

In this chapter, you will:

♦ Learn about classes

♦ Learn about `private`, `protected`, `public`, and `static` members of a class

♦ Explore how classes are implemented

♦ Learn about the various operations on classes

♦ Examine constructors and finalizers

♦ Examine the method `toString`

♦ Learn about the abstract data type (ADT)

CHAPTER 8: ASSIGNMENT COVER SHEET

Name _____   Date _____

Section _____

Lab Assignments	Grade
Lab 8.1 Defining Classes Using the Unified Modeling Language (UML) Notation	
Lab 8.2 Defining a Class that Creates an Instance of Another Class and Constructors with Parameters	
Lab 8.3 Accessing Class Members through Objects of the Class (Critical Thinking Exercise)	
Lab 8.4 Invoking Finalizers	
Lab 8.5 Overriding the Default Method toString	
Lab 8.6 Using the Abstract Data Type (Critical Thinking Exercise)	
Total Grade	

See your instructor or the introduction to this book for instructions on submitting your assignments.

Lab 8.1 Defining Classes Using the Unified Modeling Language (UML) Notation

The first step in solving problems with object-oriented design (OOD) is to identify components called objects. An object combines data and its data operations in a single unit called a class. A class is a collection of a fixed number of components. The components of a class are called the members or fields of the class. Following is the general syntax for defining a class:

```
modifier(s) class ClassIdentifier modifier(s)
{
        classMembers
}
```

In this syntax, modifier(s) are used to alter the behavior of the class, and classMembers usually consist of named constants, variable declarations, or methods. The nonstatic data members of a class are called instance variables and the member methods of a class are called the instance methods of the class.

In a class, all members are dynamic unless declared as static. A dynamic member does not allocate memory accept at instantiation using the **new** operator. Static members allocate memory at compile time. All other memory is allocated when the class is instantiated (an object is created). The members of a class are classified into four categories: private, "default," protected, and public. The "default" classification has no keyword; it is left blank. Private members cannot be accessed outside of the class. A public member is accessible outside the class. Protected and "default" members will be discussed later in this book. If a class member is declared or defined without any modifier, then that class member can be accessed from anywhere in the package.

Additionally, every class has a constructor. One type of constructor is the default constructor, which has no parameters. If a class has no constructors, Java provides the default constructor and initializes instance variables to their default values.

All Java application programs must have a main method. The controlling class has a main method. All classes that are not controlling classes have no main method. To test a non-controlling class, you must write a driver program (one that has a main method).

A class and its members can be described graphically using Unified Modeling Language (UML) notation. A UML diagram contains three boxes stacked vertically. The top box contains the name of the class, the middle box contains the data members and their data types, and the bottom box contains the member method names, parameter list, and return types. The + (plus) sign indicates that it is a public member; the - (minus) sign indicates that it is a private member. The # (pound) symbol indicates that it is a protected member.

Objectives

In this lab, you define a class with a default constructor.

After completing this lab, you will be able to:

- Use UML notation.
- Write class definitions.
- Write default constructors.
- Access class members from member methods of the class.

Estimated completion time: **50–60 minutes**

Defining Classes and Declaring Objects Using the Unified Modeling Language (UML) Notation

In this lab, you create UML diagrams, design classes using your UML diagrams, and code the classes from your designs.

1. a.   Create a UML diagram for a class named MyDate that will contain data members and a constructor that meet the criteria in the following list. This class is used to initialize instance variables.

   - The nonstatic integer data members named month, day, and year should be private members so that they cannot be directly manipulated outside of the class.

   - The nonstatic Boolean data member named good should be a public member so that it can be accessed outside of the class.

   - The constructor MyDate() should assign to the member variables the values 1 to month, 1 to day, and 2006 to year and the value true to good.

1. b.   Use your UML diagram to design a class called MyDate. Your design should be a list describing what happens at each line in the code, or should use the format your instructor requires.

1. c.   Write the Java class MyDate based on the UML diagram and the design you created in Exercises 1a and 1b. Enter your class and name it **MyDate.java**. Compile your class to be used later. (You cannot run your class code now because you have not written a program to test the operations of the class MyDate.) In Chapters 6 and 7, you created a jpfpatpd sub-folder on your system to store the files from your textbook. In that folder, create a folder named **Ch08**. In the Ch08 folder, create a folder named **Ch8ClassDef**. Save the following classes in the Ch8ClassDef folder (or use a location designated by your instructor).

   - Checks.java
   - Exchange.java
   - Money.java

   - MyDate.java
   - MyDatef.java
   - MyDatets.java

2. a.   Create a UML diagram for a class named Money that will contain data members. This class is used to identify the type of currency by a character code and amount. The nonstatic char data member named currencyType and a double data member named currencyAmount should be public members so that they can be accessed outside of the class.

2. b.   Use your UML diagram to design a class called Money. Your design should be a list of comments or should use the format your instructor requires.

2. c.   Write the Java class named Money based on the UML diagram and the design you created in Exercises 2a and 2b. Enter your class and name it **Money.java**. Compile your class to be used later. (You cannot run your class code now because you have not written a program to test the operations of the class Money.)

LAB 8.2 DEFINING A CLASS THAT CREATES AN INSTANCE OF ANOTHER CLASS AND CONSTRUCTORS WITH PARAMETERS

Once a class is defined, you can declare a reference variable of that class type. When you instantiate an object, the constructor is automatically called. The constructor called depends on the argument list and the constructor parameter list. If the argument list does not match the formal parameters of any constructor (in the order given), Java uses type conversion and looks for the best match. If no match is found, you receive a compile time error. The instance variables of the object can be initialized in a specific way by the constructor.

To access a public class member outside of the class, you use the class variable name with the member name. The syntax is to separate the reference variable and the member name by a dot, called the dot operator or member access operator.

Objectives

In this lab, you use a class in a driver program.

After completing this lab, you will be able to:

- Write a class with instance variable fields of a user-defined class.

- Write constructors with parameters.

Estimated completion time: **50–60 minutes**

Defining a Class that Creates an Instance of Another Class and Constructors with Parameters

In the following exercises, you update your UML diagram and change the design and code of your programs.

1. a.   Update your UML diagram for the class MyDate. Add a MyDate constructor with parameters for month, day, and year to assign values to the instance variables. Add a method printDate() to display the date. You also need a method to validate the date. In programming, validation means that the values are in a range that could be valid. For example, a month value must be between 1 and 12. It does not mean that the data is correct, only valid.

   The UML diagram should meet the following criteria:

   - The constructor MyDate() is passed three integer variables as parameters and assigns these values to the integer data members month, day, and year, and assigns the value false to good. The constructor MyDate() should call the method validate() to make sure that the instance variables contain valid values.

   - The member method named printDate() is void, has no formal parameters, and should be a public member so that it can be accessed outside of the class. The member method printDate() should display the date in the format mm-dd-yyyy.

   - The member method named validate() is void, has no formal parameters, and should be a private member so that it can only be accessed within the class. The method validate() should check to make sure that the values for month are between 1 and 12, the values for day are within the range for the appropriate month, and the value for year is greater than 0. The member method validate() should either display the message "You entered a valid date" or "You entered an invalid date." It should then call the method printDate().

1. b. Add to your design of the class MyDate using the changes in your UML diagram. Your changes should be a list describing what happens at each line in the code, or should use the format your instructor requires.

1. c.   Write in Java the class MyDate based on the new UML diagram and the new design you created in Exercises 1a and 1b. Make the changes to your code **MyDate.java**. Compile your class to be used later.

2. a.   *Critical Thinking Exercise*: Create a UML diagram for a class named Exchange that will contain data members and member methods that meet the criteria in the following list. This class is used to input, validate, and convert Mexican pesos, Euro dollars, and Swiss francs to U.S. dollars.

   ■   Create instance variable fields named sum and starting. These variables should be Money data types that you defined in Lab 8.1. These data members should be private members so that they cannot be directly manipulated outside of the class. The data member starting will contain the starting currency amount and type of currency. The data member sum will contain the amount converted into U. S. dollars. Remember to use the **new** operator when creating objects.

   ■   The nonstatic Boolean data member named more should be a public member so that it can be accessed outside of the class. The data member named more will contain true or false depending on whether the user wants to continue processing.

   ■   The void method setAmount() has no formal parameters and should be a private method. The method setAmount() asks the user to enter the starting amount of money. If the user does not enter a positive value, the method should loop until a positive value is entered. Because the method setAmount() asks users for a value, it must throw an exception.

   ■   The void method setType() has no formal parameters and should be a private method. The method setType() asks the user to enter the type of money—d for U.S. dollars, p for Mexican pesos, f for Swiss francs, e for Euro dollars, or q to quit. If the user does not enter a valid type, the method should loop until a valid type is entered. If the user enters 'd,' 'p,' 'f,' or 'e,' the method setAmount() should be called. If the user enters 'q,' the data member more is set to false to allow the user to quit. Because the method setType() asks users for a value, it must throw an exception.

   ■   The void method convert() has no formal parameters and should be a private method. The method convert() calculates the U. S. dollar equivalent of the starting.currencyAmount and assigns that value to sum.currencyAmount. Use the following exchange rates for your calculation:

      1 dollar = 1.4054 Swiss francs

      1 dollar = 0.9553 Euro dollars

      1 dollar = 9.815 Mexican pesos

- The void method outputType() has no formal parameters and should be a private method. The method outputType() outputs the string name associated with the currencyType. This string will be part of another output message and needs to begin and end with a blank character. Use the following messages:

    If currencyType is 'd,' output the string " U. S. dollars ".

    If currencyType is 'p,' output the string " Mexican pesos ".

    If currencyType is 'e,' output the string " Euro dollars ".

    If currency Type is 'f,' output the string " Swiss francs ".

- The void method displayStart() has no formal parameters and should be a private method. The method displayStart() checks startingType and outputs a message depending on the startingType. The string output appears as follows:

    You're starting with *amount* in *currency type*

    In this output, *amount* is the starting amount entered by the user and *currency type* is either U. S. dollars, Euro dollars, Swiss francs, or Mexican pesos.

- The Boolean method setData() has no formal parameters and should be a public member. The method setData() should call the method setType(). If the data member more is true and the value of the data member starting type is not equal to 'd,' the method convert() is called. If the data member more is true, the method displayStart() is called. Because the method setData() calls methods containing input, it must throw an exception.

- The default constructor Exchange() initializes the Boolean value more to true and calls the method setData() to initialize the starting currency amount and the starting currency type. Because setData returns a Boolean value, it must declare a local variable temp in the constructor Exchange() and set temp to the value returned from the call to the method SetData(). Because the constructor Exchange() calls a method that calls other methods containing input, it must throw an exception.

2. b. Design a class named Exchange based on your UML diagram. Your design should be a list describing what happens at each line in the code, or should use the format your instructor requires.

2. c.   Write the Java class named Exchange based on the UML diagram and the design you created in Exercises 2a and 2b. Enter your class and name it **Exchange.java**. Compile your class to be used later.

LAB 8.3 ACCESSING CLASS MEMBERS THROUGH OBJECTS OF THE CLASS

To allocate memory for the instance variables of the class, you must create an object of the class using the operator **new**. The general syntax for using the operator **new** follows:

```
new className()
```

or

```
new className(argument1, argument2, ..., argumentN)
```

The class allows you to perform built-in operations on data members within the class. You cannot perform arithmetic operations on class objects. If you use relational operators to compare two class objects, you are comparing reference variables.

To test your classes, you must import them into your driver program. You can create packages and categorize your classes. Check with your instructor regarding where you should save your compiled classes to be imported into your driver program. To create a package and add a class to the package so that the class can be used in a program, you complete the following tasks:

- Define the class to be public. If the class is not public, it can be used only within the package.

- Choose a name for the package.

Objectives

In this lab, you use a class in a driver program.

After completing this lab, you will be able to:

- Instantiate an object of a class.

- Access public class members through objects of the class.

- Access class members from member methods of the class.

- Create a package of class files.

- Import user-defined classes.

Estimated completion time: **50–60 minutes**

Accessing Class Members through Objects of the Class

In the following exercises, you create a package of class files, and then design and create a driver program.

1. Create a package of the class files that you created in this chapter. Complete the following steps to create the package.

- Create a classes folder on your hard disk (or use the name and location specified by your instructor). In this folder, create a folder named jpfpatpd.

- In jpfpatpd, create a subfolder ch08.

- In ch08, create a subfolder Ch8ClassDef.

- Add the following statement at the beginning of each class file:

```
package jpfpatpd.ch08.Ch8ClassDef
```

- Save these files in the Ch8ClassDef folder and compile each Java file.

2. a.   Design a driver program that imports the MyDate class you created in Lab 8.1. This program is designed to test your class. Your main method should prompt the user with the message "Please enter today's date (month, day, and year separated by spaces):" and instantiate an object of the MyDate class named today using the values input as arguments to the MyDate constructor. Write your design in the following space provided.

2. b.   Write a Java program based on the design you created in Exercise 2a. Include the following import statement:

```
import jpfpatpd.ch08.Ch8ClassDef.*;
```

For readability, insert blank lines to separate parts of the program. Include comments to explain the different sections of code.

Save the program as **AssnDate.java** in the Chap08 folder on your Student Disk. Compile, execute, and test the program with several sets of data to test your class.

Following is a copy of the screen results that might appear after running your program several times, depending on the data entered. The input entered by the user appears in bold.

```
This program is a date validator.
When you enter a date, it will tell you
whether the date is a valid date. You must enter
a year greater than 0.

Please enter today's date (month, day, and year separated by spaces):
11 23 2005
You entered a valid date 11-23-2005
This program is a date validator.
When you enter a date, it will tell you
whether the date is a valid date. You must enter
a year greater than 0.
Please enter today's date (month, day, and year separated by spaces):
2 31 2004
You entered an invalid date
This program is a date validator.
When you enter a date, it will tell you
```

```
whether the date is a valid date. You must enter
a year greater than 0.
Please enter today's date (month, day, and year separated by spaces):
13 23 2006
You entered an invalid date
```

3. a. *Critical Thinking Exercise*: Design a driver program that imports the Exchange class you created in Lab 8.2. After instantiating an object of the Exchange class, test to see whether the user chose to quit by testing the instance variable more. If the user chose to quit, display the message "You quit the program before entering any data." Write a loop that is executed as long as the instance variable more is true. Call the Exchange class method setData() until the user chooses to quit. Write your design in the space provided.

3. b. Write a Java program based on the design you created in Exercise 3a. For readability, insert blank lines to separate parts of the program. Include comments to explain the different sections of code.

Save the program as **MoneyEx.java** in the Chap08 folder on your Student Disk. Compile, execute, and test the program with several sets of data to test your class. Choose to quit as the first entry for your first run. Then run the program again making different selections.

Following is a copy of the screen results that might appear, depending on the data entered. The input entered by the user appears in bold.

If the user enters q for the first selection, the program displays the following messages:

```
This is a money changer program.
If you enter the type of money,
(d) for U. S. dollars, (p) for Mexican pesos,
(f) for Swiss francs, (e) for Euro dollars,
or (q) to quit, I will tell you the value
in U. S. dollars.
q
You quit the program before entering any data.
```

If the program is run again and q is not the first selection, the following messages should be displayed:

```
This is a money changer program.
If you enter the type of money,
(d) for U. S. dollars, (p) for Mexican pesos,
(f) for Swiss francs, (e) for Euro dollars,
or (q) to quit, I will tell you the value
in U. S. dollars.

Enter type of money (d) for U.S. dollars, (p) for Mexican pesos,
(f) for Swiss francs, (e) for Euro dollars or (q)uit: d
Starting amount: 1000
You're starting with 1000 in U. S. dollars.

Enter type of money (d) for U.S. dollars, (p) for Mexican pesos,
(f) for Swiss francs, (e) for Euro dollars or (q)uit: p
Starting amount: 103.94
Your starting amount of 103.94 in Mexican pesos is 10.59 in U. S. dollars.

Enter type of money (d) for U.S. dollars, (p) for Mexican pesos,
(f) for Swiss francs, (e) for Euro dollars or (q)uit: f
Starting amount: 73.46
Your starting amount of 73.46 in Swiss francs is 52.27 in U. S. dollars.

Enter type of money (d) for U.S. dollars, (p) for Mexican pesos,
(f) for Swiss francs, (e) for Euro dollars or (q)uit: e
Starting amount: 459
Your starting amount of 459 in Euro dollars is 480.48 in U. S. dollars.

Enter type of money (d) for U.S. dollars, (p) for Mexican pesos,
(f) for Swiss francs, (e) for Euro dollars or (q)uit: q
```

LAB 8.4 INVOKING FINALIZERS

A finalizer is another tool written like a method, but is not technically a method, and is available in a class. Although rarely used in Java programs, finalizers are presented here for informational purposes and to help you understand memory allocation. The finalizer is written using the name finalize(), is protected (discussed later), and has no parameters. Furthermore, there can be only one finalizer per class. The finalizer automatically executes when no valid reference points to the class object, although there is no guarantee that a finalizer will be called. However, before the garbage collector is run, Java calls finalizers. To ensure that your finalizer is called and that your object has been dereferenced, include the following statements at the end of your test program:

```
objectName = null
System.gc();
```

Objectives

In this lab, you define a finalizer of a class.

After completing this lab, you will be able to:

■ Write a finalizer for a class.

Estimated completion time: **15–20 minutes**

Invoking Finalizers

In the following exercises, you update your UML diagram and change the design and code of your programs.

1. a. Update your UML diagram for your class MyDate renaming the class to MyDatef. Add a finalizer that displays the message **Mydate object finalizer:** *mm-dd-yyyy*, where *mm-dd-yyyy* is the value of the object.

1. b.   Update the design of your class MyDate based on the changes in your UML diagram of MyDatef. Your design should be a list describing what happens at each line in the code, or should use the format your instructor requires.

1. c.   Write the class MyDatef based on the changes in your UML diagram and design in Exercises 1a and 1b. Compile your class.

1. d.   Add code to your AssnDate.java program to ensure that the finalizer is called. Save the program as **AssnDatef.java** in the Chap08 folder on your Student Disk. Compile, execute, and test the program.

Following is a copy of the screen results that might appear after running your program several times, depending on the data entered. The input entered by the user appears in bold.

```
This program is a date validator.
When you enter a date, it will tell you
whether the date is a valid date. You must enter
a year greater than 0.

Please enter today's date (month, day, and year separated by spaces):
11 23 2006
You entered a valid date 11-23-2006

MyDatef object finalizer: 11-23-2006
```

LAB 8.5 OVERRIDING THE DEFAULT METHOD toString

In Java, every class is a subclass of the class Object. As such, the methods of the class Object are inherited. The method toString() is a method of the class Object and is used to convert an object to a String object. The method toString() is public, does not take any parameters, and returns a String object. You can override the default definition of any method by including another method of the same name and signature in the class. The definition of that method will then be called instead of the default method.

Objectives

In this lab, you define a method toString() to override the default toString() method.

After completing this lab, you will be able to:

■ Write a method to override the toString() default method.

Estimated completion time: **15–20 minutes**

Overriding the Default Method toString

In the following exercises, you update your UML diagram and class design, and then revise the MyDate class.

1. a. Update the UML diagram you created for your class MyDatef renaming the class to MyDatets. Add a toString() method.

    The member method named toString() is void, has no formal parameters, returns a String object, and should be a public member so that it can be accessed outside of the class.

1. b. Update the design of your class MyDate based on the changes in your UML diagram of MyDatets. Your design should be a list describing what happens at each line in the code, or should use the format your instructor requires.

1. c. Write the class MyDatets based on the changes in your UML diagram and design in Exercises 1a and 1b. Compile your class.

1. d. Add code to your AssnDate.java program to call the println() method with only the MyDate object. Save the program as **AssnDatets.java** in the Chap08 folder on your Student Disk. Compile, execute, and test the program.

Following is a copy of the screen results that might appear after running your program several times, depending on the data entered. The input entered by the user appears in bold.

```
This program is a date validator.
When you enter a date, it will tell you
whether the date is a valid date. You must enter
a year greater than 0.

Please enter today's date (month, day, and year separated by spaces):
11 23 2006
You entered a valid date 11-23-2006

MyDatets object finalizer: 11-23-2006
```

Lab 8.6 Using the Abstract Data Type and Information Hiding

Separating the design details from their use is called abstraction. An abstract data type (ADT) is a concept, not a real data type, that specifies the logical properties of data without including the implementation details. Hiding the implementation details (information hiding) ensures that an object will be used in exactly the same way throughout the project.

When you instantiate objects of a class, only nonstatic data members of the class become the data members of each object. For each static member of the class, Java allocates only one memory space. All objects of that class refer to the same memory space.

Objectives

In this lab, you create your own abstract data type using classes.

After completing this lab, you will be able to:

- Write a program using an abstract data type with static and nonstatic data members.

Estimated completion time: **120–150 minutes**

Using the Abstract Data Type and Information Hiding

In the following exercises, you create a UML diagram for a new program, and then design and write the program.

1. a. *Critical Thinking Exercise*: A traveler wants to purchase a number of traveler's checks, each having a set amount for four different curriencies: Mexican pesos, Euro dollars, Swiss francs, and U. S. dollars. The traveler wants to know the value of all traveler's checks in U. S. dollars. When the traveler makes a purchase, he withdraws a designated number of travelers checks of a particular type. Additionally, this transaction should be refused if there are not sufficient travelers checks of the type designated.

   The traveler can increase the number of traveler's checks by making a deposit, but cannot change the amount established for the amount of the check once it has been established.

   Create a UML diagram for a class named Checks that will contain data members and member methods that meet the criteria cited in the problem statement above.

   Create a class Checks that includes the following members:

   - The nonstatic integer data member named numberOfChecks to keep track of the number of traveler's checks available.

   - The nonstatic integer data member named faceAmount to keep track of the face value of the traveler's checks available.

   - The nonstatic character data member named countryCode to keep track of the type of traveler's check being processed.

   - The static double data member named balance to keep track of the total value of all traveler's checks in U. S. dollars.

   - The integer method getCount() to return the number of traveler's checks of a particular type.

   - The integer method getAmount() to return the face value of traveler's checks of a particular type.

   - The double method getBalance() to return the U. S. dollar amount of all traveler's checks.

- The void method Deposit() to add or increase the number of traveler's checks of a particular type. The first time a deposit is made, the face amount of the traveler's check is set. The balance is updated to include new deposits of traveler's checks. Each check for a particular kind of currency has the same face value. Purchases can only be made in terms of checks and *not* in terms of amount of currency.

- The void method cashCheck() to decrease the number of traveler's checks of a particular type. If no face amount has been set or if there are not enough traveler's checks of a particular type, display a message to the user and do not process the request. The balance is updated to include new withdrawals of traveler's checks.

- The void method convert() to convert the deposit or withdrawal amount to U. S. dollars.

1. b.   Design a class named Checks based on your UML diagram. Your design should be a list describing what happens at each line in the code, or should use the format your instructor requires.

1. c. Write the class Checks based on the UML diagram and the design you created in Exercises 1a and 1b. Enter your class and name it **Checks.java**. Compile your class to be used later.

2. Design a driver program that imports the Checks class you implemented in Exercise 1. Your main method should use a grid layout that was introduced in Chapter 6 for the user to select either Mexican peso, Swiss franc, Euro dollar, U. S. dollar, Check Balance, or Exit.

   If the user selects a currency type, use an input dialog box to ask the user to enter either a deposit or withdrawal, or to quit.

   The first time a user selects a deposit of a particular type, the user should be instructed to enter the number of checks and the face amount of the check to be deposited. Otherwise, the user should only be asked to enter the number of checks. The balance of the traveler's checks should be updated by the equivalent amount of the deposit in U. S. dollars.

   If the user enters a withdrawal, the user should be notified if there has never been a deposit of a particular type. Additionally, the user should be notified if the number of traveler's checks is not available for the amount requested. The balance of the traveler's checks should be updated by the equivalent amount of the deposit in U. S. dollars.

   When the user selects quit, a message box should appear to inform the user that the check cashing is complete.

   Save the program as **TravlChk.java** in the Chap08 folder on your Student Disk. Compile, execute, and test the program with several sets of data to test your class. Following is a copy of the screen results that might appear after running your program.

Figure 8-1   Traveler's Check Machine dialog box

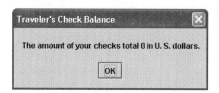

Figure 8-2   Traveler's Check Balance dialog box

Figure 8-3   No Checks Available dialog box

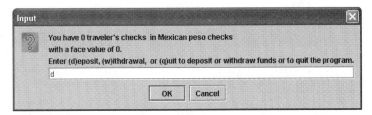

Figure 8-4   Checking the number of Mexican peso checks

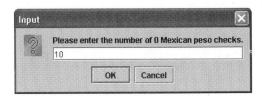

Figure 8-5   Entering the number of Mexican peso checks

Figure 8-6   Purchasing Mexican peso checks

Figure 8-7   Calculating the amount of Mexican peso checks

Figure 8-8   Checking the number of Swiss franc checks

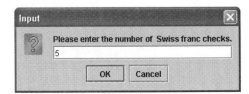

Figure 8-9   Entering the number of Swiss franc checks

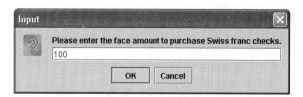

Figure 8-10   Purchasing Swiss franc checks

Figure 8-11   Calculating the amount of Mexican peso checks

Either copy the grid and dialog boxes that appear and paste them into a document or print the screens of the grid and dialog boxes.

ARRAYS AND STRINGS

In this chapter, you will:

♦ Learn about arrays
♦ Explore how to declare and manipulate data into arrays
♦ Understand the meaning of "array index out of bounds"
♦ Become familiar with the restrictions on array processing
♦ Discover how to pass an array as a parameter to a method
♦ Discover how to manipulate data in a two-dimensional array
♦ Learn about multidimensional arrays

CHAPTER 9: ASSIGNMENT COVER SHEET

Name _____   Date _____

Section _____

Lab Assignments	Grade
Lab 9.1 Declaring and Processing Arrays	
Lab 9.2 Checking Index Bounds and Initializing Arrays	
Lab 9.3 Passing Arrays as Parameters to Methods (Critical Thinking Exercise)	
Lab 9.4 Coding with Parallel Arrays and with an Array of Objects	
Lab 9.5 Manipulating Data in a Two-Dimensional Array (Critical Thinking Exercise)	
Total Grade	

See your instructor or the introduction to this book for instructions on submitting your assignments.

LAB 9.1 DECLARING AND PROCESSING ARRAYS

An array is an object that is a collection of a fixed number of variables, wherein all of the variables are of the same data type. Arrays are accessed through reference variables like all other objects (except String). The general syntax to declare a one-dimensional array is:

```
dataType[] arrayName;
```

Note that Java accepts declarations as `dataType arrayName[];` but this syntax is not standard.

The general syntax to instantiate an array object is:

```
arrayName = new dataType[intExp];
```

At instantiation, the value in the square brackets indicates the number of components of the array. Java automatically initializes array components to their default values at instantiation.

To access a component of the array, you also use an expression that evaluates to a non-negative integer that appears inside the brackets and indicates the position from the beginning of the array. Do not confuse the size at declaration with the position from the beginning of the array. Additionally, the size of the array does not need to be specified at compile time. If the size of an array is determined during program execution, it is called a dynamic array.

Working with arrays almost always requires iteration. An array component is treated the same as any individual variable. Operations are the same for individual components as for an operation on any variable.

For example, the following code would assign the fourth variable in an array to the variable num:

```
int [] array = new int [5];
int num;
num = array[3];
```

After instantiation, a public instance variable length is associated with each array, and contains the size of the array.

Objectives

In this lab, you declare, instantiate, and process the components of an array.

After completing this lab, you will be able to:

- Declare and instantiate a one-dimensional array object.

- Specify an array size during program execution.

- Process a one-dimensional array.

- Access individual array elements.

Estimated completion time: **50–60 minutes**

Declaring and Processing Arrays

In the following exercises, you design and write programs using arrays.

1. a. Design a program to record the weekly sales for each salesperson of a company. Each salesperson is identified by a number, 1–5. Ask the user for the salesperson's number, also called the sales number, and for the amount of sales to be entered. Because the program will use the salesperson's number as the array index for storing the sales amount, check to be sure that the index is valid.

The user can enter the sales number and amount of sales in any order. After all sales values have been entered, print the sales in a table that shows the sales number order, the total amount of sales, and the total of sales.

Following is a copy of the screen results that might appear after running your program, depending on the data entered. The input entered by the user is shown in bold.

```
This is a sales tracking program.
You will enter the number of salespersons, the salesperson
identification number, and the amount of sales.
The sales and total sales will be displayed.

Enter the number of salespersons to be processed.
5
Enter the sales number and amount of sales separated by a space.
5 340.50
Enter the sales number and amount of sales separated by a space.
1 275.75
Enter the sales number and amount of sales separated by a space.
2 0
Enter the sales number and amount of sales separated by a space.
4 225
Enter the sales number and amount of sales separated by a space.
3 175.50

                    Weekly Sales by Salesperson

1       2       3       4       5
275.75  0.00    175.50  225.00  340.50
Total Sales:    1016.75
```

Write your design in the following space. Your design should be a list describing what happens at each line in the program, or should use the format your instructor requires.

1. b. Write a Java program based on the design that you created in Exercise 1a. Save the program as **Sales.java** in the Chap09 folder on your Student Disk, and then compile, run, and test the program. Copy the instructions, input, and output that are displayed, and paste them in a block comment at the end of your program. Then print your program to submit with your work.

LAB 9.2 CHECKING INDEX BOUNDS AND INITIALIZING ARRAYS

An array can be initialized at declaration by placing the values between braces separated by commas. If the size of the array is not indicated at declaration, it defaults to the number of values in the initialization block. If an array is declared and initialized at the same time, do not use the new operator to instantiate the array object.

For example an array with no initialization is defined as follows:

```
dataType[] arrayName;
arrayName = new dataType [intExp];
or combined
dataType[] arrayName = new dataType[intExp];
```

When an array with initialization at declaration is defined as follows:

```
dataType[] arrayName = {value1, value2, value3, …, valuen};
```

The array is of size n.

If an array index goes out of bounds during program execution, it throws an ArrayIndexOutOfBoundsException exception. Remember that array variables are accessed with the index values 0 through the size of the index minus one. One common error is to use the array size as an index. For instance the following is an error:

```
int[] array = new int[5];
array[5] = 24;
```

To copy the values of one array into another, you would need to copy each value:

```
int[] arrayA = new int[5];
int[] arrayB = new int[5];
for (int index = 0; index < 5; index++)
    arrayA[index] =  arrayB[index];
```

For deep copying, operations must be done one component at a time, which is called component-wise in programming.

Objectives

In this lab, you check to see that an index value is in bounds and initialize an array at declaration.

After completing this lab, you will be able to:

- Check for array index out of bounds.

- Initialize arrays at declaration.

Estimated completion time: **40–50 minutes**

Checking Index Bounds and Initializing Arrays

In the following exercises, you design and write a program that initializes an array at declaration and checks array indices to make sure they are in bounds.

1. a.   Design a program for a trucking company that has seven trucks in its fleet. Each truck is identified by a number from one to seven. Each truck also has a maximum weight allowance, which has already been determined. Assign the maximum weight limit to each truck at initialization. Before a truck can begin its route, it must be weighed to see if it falls within its weight allowance.

Ask the user for the truck number and the loaded weight. Display a message indicating whether the truck falls in the allowable weight limit. Use the following values as maximum weight limits and enter the weigh-in values for each truck:

Truck number	Maximum weight limit	Truck weigh-in
1	50,000	45,000
2	25,000	30,000
3	20,000	20,000
4	35,000	30,000
5	40,000	35,000
6	25,000	27,000
7	30,000	20,000

Following are copies of the dialog boxes that might appear after running your program, depending on the data entered.

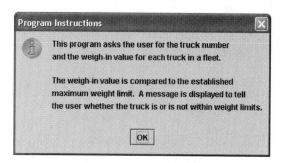

Figure 9-1   Program Instructions dialog box

Figure 9-2   Truck Number Input dialog box

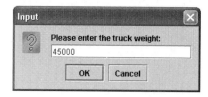

Figure 9-3   Truck Weight Input dialog box

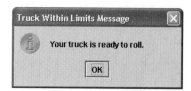

Figure 9-4   Truck Within Limits Message dialog box

Figure 9-5   Truck Number Input dialog box

Figure 9-6   Truck Weight Input dialog box

Figure 9-7   Truck Excess Weight Message dialog box

Figure 9-8   Truck Number Input dialog box

Figure 9-9   Truck Weight Input dialog box

Figure 9-10   Truck Within Limits Message dialog box

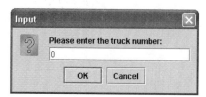

Figure 9-11 Truck Number Input dialog box

Figure 9-12 Incorrect Truck Number Message dialog box

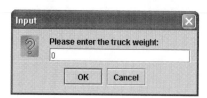

Figure 9-13 Truck Weight Input dialog box

Figure 9-14 Incorrect Truck Weight Message dialog box

Figure 9-15 Truck Weigh-In Complete dialog box

Write your design in the following space. Your design should be a list describing what happens at each line in the program, or should use the format your instructor requires.

1. b.   Write a Java program based on the design that you created in Exercise 1a. Save the program as **Trucks.java** in the Chap09 folder on your Student Disk, and then compile, run, and test the program. Either copy the grid and dialog boxes that appear and paste them into a document or print the screens of the grid and dialog boxes. Then print your program to submit with your work.

LAB 9.3 PASSING ARRAYS AS PARAMETERS TO METHODS

Like other objects, arrays can be passed as parameters to methods. If all elements of an array are not used, the number of variables in the array to be processed should also be passed to the method.

The name of the array used to identify the array is a reference to the array. Used by itself, it is the memory address of the first component of the array. In other words, the value contained in the reference of the array is the memory address of the first component of the array. When you pass an array as a parameter, the base address of the actual array is passed to the formal parameter.

Objectives

In this lab, you initialize an array at declaration, and use an array as an argument to a method.

After completing this lab, you will be able to:

- Initialize a Boolean array.

- Use arrays as actual arguments to methods.

Estimated completion time: **80–90 minutes**

Passing Arrays as Parameters to Methods

In the following exercises, you design and write a program that passes an array to a method as a parameter.

1. a. *Critical Thinking Exercise*: Design a program to search an array for letters that the user enters. Declare a Boolean array of size 26 to represent each letter of the alphabet. (Remember that the alphabet contains 52 characters if you count uppercase and lowercase. You must convert your characters to the same case.) You do not need to initialize this array to false at declaration because false is the default value when a Boolean array is initialized. If the program finds a letter in the array that the user entered, change the array element that matches the alphabetic character by position to true.

    Call a method to check for the letter in the array and to count the number of occurrences of the letter being checked. Output the number of occurrences of that letter. Call a method to display which letters of the alphabet have been found in the array.

    Following is a copy of the screen results that might appear after running your program, depending on the data entered. The input entered by the user is in bold.

    ```
    This is a program that counts each time a
    letter in the alphabet occurs in a word.

    Please enter a word: howdy
    The word howdy has 5 characters.

    What letter would you like to guess? (Enter zero to quit.) a
    There are 0 A's.

    What letter would you like to guess? (Enter zero to quit.) b
    There are 0 B's.

    What letter would you like to guess? (Enter zero to quit.) c
    There are 0 C's.

    What letter would you like to guess? (Enter zero to quit.) d
    There are 1 D's.
    ```

```
What letter would you like to guess? (Enter zero to quit.) e
There are 0 E's.

What letter would you like to guess? (Enter zero to quit.) f
There are 0 F's.

What letter would you like to guess? (Enter zero to quit.) g
There are 0 G's.

What letter would you like to guess? (Enter zero to quit.) h
There are 1 H's.

What letter would you like to guess? (Enter zero to quit.) 0
You found these letters:
D
H
```

Write your design in the following space. Your design should be a list describing what happens at each line in the program, or should use the format your instructor requires.

1. b.   Write a Java program based on the design that you created in Exercise 1a. Save the program as **countLet.java** in the Chap09 folder on your Student Disk, and then compile, run, and test the program. Copy the instructions, input, and output that are displayed, and paste them in a block comment at the end of your program. Then print your program to submit with your work.

LAB 9.4 CODING WITH PARALLEL ARRAYS

Parallel arrays are two or more arrays whose corresponding components hold related information. If you need to keep track of multiple items for the same topic, you can create more than one array where the information is related by the placement within the arrays.

You can also use arrays to manipulate objects. The syntax for an array of objects is:

```
Class[] reference = new Class[size];
```

This statement only creates an array of references. Only one object, the array itself, is instantiated from this statement, unless you use this statement to create an array of Strings.

Objectives

In this lab, you process parallel arrays and an array of objects.

After completing this lab, you will be able to:

- Process parallel arrays.

- Process an array of objects.

Estimated completion time: **60–90 minutes**

Coding with Parallel Arrays

In the following exercises, you design and write a program that uses parallel arrays, create a UML diagram for the program, and design and write a class based on the UML diagram. Then you design a driver program that imports the class you wrote.

1. a. Design a program to keep track of the hits, walks, and outs of a baseball team. Use parallel arrays to keep track of each player's accumulated statistics. The player number is the index of the array. Ask the user for the player number, hits, walks, and outs for each game. Enter data for multiple games with nine batters per game. The team has 20 players, but only nine will have statistics for a particular game.

   Display the accumulated hits, walks, and outs for all players for the season.

   Following is a copy of some of the screen results that might appear after running your program, depending on the data entered. The instructions should resemble the following when you use the input given.

   ```
   This program asks the user for a baseball player's number,
   and his number of hits, walks, and outs for five games.
   Only nine players bat each game.

   For game 1, enter the player number: 1
   Enter the hits for game 1 for player 1: 2
   Enter the walks for game 1 for player 1: 2
   Enter the outs for game 1 for player 1: 2
   ```

   Test using the following input:

   ```
   1  2  2  2
   20  0  5  1
   2  0  0  6
   18  4  2  0
   3  2  1  3
   4  1  2  3
   7  0  0  3
   ```

```
8  1  4  1
9  3  2  1
10  2  2  2
11  6  0  0
12  2  2  2
2  0  5  1
20  0  0  6
17  4  2  0
4  2  1  3
3  1  2  3
7  0  0  3
8  1  4  1
9  3  2  1
16  2  2  2
11  6  0  0
1  2  2  2
20  0  5  1
2  0  0  6
18  4  2  0
13  2  1  3
14  1  2  3
17  0  0  3
3  1  4  1
7  3  2  1
4  2  2  2
6  6  0  0
5  2  2  2
2  0  5  1
20  0  0  6
8  4  2  0
3  2  1  3
14  1  2  3
17  0  0  3
18  1  4  1
19  3  2  1
11  2  2  2
13  6  0  0
15  0  0  1
```

The output should resemble the following code.

Player	Hits	Walks	Outs
1	4	4	4
2	0	10	14
3	6	8	10
4	5	5	8
5	2	2	2
6	6	0	0
7	3	2	7
8	6	10	2
9	6	4	2
10	2	2	2
11	14	2	2
12	2	2	2
13	8	1	3
14	2	4	6
15	0	0	1
16	2	2	2
17	4	2	6
18	9	8	1
19	3	2	1
20	0	10	14

Write your design in the following space. Your design should be a list describing what happens at each line in the program, or should use the format your instructor requires.

1. b. Write a Java program based on the design that you created in Exercise 1a. Save the program as **Baseball.java** in the Chap09 folder on your Student Disk, and then compile, run, and test the program. Copy the instructions, input, and output that are displayed, and paste them in a block comment at the end of your program. Then print your program to submit with your work.

2. a. Create a UML diagram for a class named PlayBall that contains data members and member methods that meet the criteria cited in the Exercise 1a problem statement.

2. b. Design a class named PlayBall based on your UML diagram. Your design should be a list describing what happens at each line in the code, or should use the format your instructor requires.

2. c.   Write in Java the class PlayBall based on the UML diagram and the design you created in Exercises 2a and 2b. Enter your class and name it **PlayBall.java**. Compile your class to be used later.

3. a.   Design a driver program that imports the PlayBall class you implemented in Exercise 2. Ask the user for the number of players on the team, though only nine will have statistics for a particular game. Also ask the user for the number of games in the season.

Use an array of the type PlayBall as defined in Exercise 2. Your array will be the size of the number of players on the team as entered by the user. You will accumulate all the hits, runs, and walks for all games of the season. The user will input the number of games for the season.

Display the accumulated hits, walks, and outs for all players for the season.

Following is a copy of some of the instructions that should appear when running your program.

```
This program tracks a baseball player's number, and his
number of hits, walks, and outs for each game in a season.
Only nine players bat each game.

How many players are on your team? 20
How many games are played this season? 5

For game 1, enter the player number (-1 to quit): 1
Enter the hits for game 1 for player 1: 2
Enter the walks for game 1 for player 1: 2
Enter the outs for game 1 for player 1: 2
```

Write your design in the following space. Your design should be a list describing what happens at each line in the program, or should use the format your instructor requires.

3. b. Write a Java program based on the design that you created in Exercise 3a. Save the program as **Basebal2.java** in the Chap09 folder on your Student Disk, and then compile, run, and test the program with the same data used in Exercise 2. Copy the instructions, input, and output that are displayed, and paste them in a block comment at the end of your program. Then print your program to submit with your work.

LAB 9.5 MANIPULATING DATA IN A TWO-DIMENSIONAL AND A MULTIDIMENSIONAL ARRAY

In the previous lab, you manipulated parallel arrays and arrays of objects. Because all data types were the same, you could manipulate the data in table form by using a two-dimensional array. The syntax for declaring a two-dimensional array is:

```
dataType[][] arrayName;
```

The general syntax to instantiate a two-dimensional array object is:

```
arrayName = new dataType[intExp1][intExp2];
```

The expression intExp1 specifies the number of rows and the expression intExp2 specifies the number of columns in the array.

Java allows you to specify a different number of columns for each row, called ragged arrays. In this case, each row must be instantiated separately. The syntax would be:

```
dataType[][] arrayName;
arrayName = new dataType[]; //Create the number of rows
arrayName[0] = new int[cols];  //Create the columns for the first row.
```

A two-dimensional array can be processed in three ways:

1. Process the entire array.

2. Process a particular row of the array, called row processing.

3. Process a particular column of the array, called column processing.

A collection of a fixed number of elements arranged in *n* dimensions where *n* is greater than or equal to 1 is called an n-dimensional array. The general syntax for declaring and instantiating an n-dimensional array is:

```
dataType[][]...[] arrayName
        = new dataType[intExp1][intExp2]...[intExpn];
```

Objectives

In this lab, you declare, instantiate, and process the components of an array.

After completing this lab, you will be able to:

- Declare and instantiate a two-dimensional array object.

- Process a two-dimensional array.

- Process a two-dimensional array by columns.

- Declare and instantiate a three-dimensional array object.

- Process a three-dimensional array.

- Process a three-dimensional array by column and by the third dimension.

Estimated completion time: **120–150 minutes**

Manipulating Data in a Two-Dimensional and a Multidimensional Array

In the following exercises, you use a two-dimensional array instead of parallel arrays to redesign the program you created in Lab 9.4. You also redesign the program to use a three-dimensional array.

1. a. Refer to the program design in Lab 9.4 Exercise 1. Instead of using parallel arrays, use a two-dimensional array to design a program to keep track of baseball players' hits, runs, and outs for a season. Allow the user to determine the number of players on the team and the number of games in the season. Test to be sure that there are at least nine players and one game. Display the total number of hits, walks, and outs of each player and the total of hits, walks, and outs for the team. Test your program for less than nine players, and then test using the same data listed in Lab 9.4 Exercise 1.

Following is a copy of some of the instructions that should appear when running your program and entering fewer than nine players. The input entered by the user is shown in bold.

```
This program asks the user for a baseball player's number,
and his number of hits, walks, and outs for each game in a season.
Only nine players bat each game.

How many players are on the team?  2
You cannot play with less than 9 players!
```

When running your program using the test data from Lab 9.4 Exercise 1, your output should resemble the output shown in Lab 9.4, except for your instructions and total lines.

Following is a copy of some of the instructions that should appear when running your program. The input entered by the user is shown in bold.

```
This program asks the user for a baseball player's number,
and his number of hits, walks, and outs for each game in a season.
Only nine players bat each game.

How many players are on the team?  20
How many games are in the season?  5

For game 1 enter the player number (-1 to quit): 1
Enter the hits for game 1 for player 1: 2
Enter the walks for game 1 for player 1: 2
Enter the outs for game 1 for player 1: 2
```

The total line should resemble:

```
Totals  83       80       89
```

Write your design in the following space. Your design should be a list describing what happens at each line in the program, or should use the format your instructor requires.

1. b. Write a Java program based on the design that you created in Exercise 1a. Save the program as **Basebal3.java** in the Chap09 folder on your Student Disk, and then compile, run, and test the program. Copy the instructions, input, and output that are displayed, and paste them in a block comment at the end of your program. Then print your program to submit with your work.

2. a. *Critical Thinking Exercise*: Redesign the program you created in Exercise 1a to use a three-dimensional array. Instead of using columns as accumulators for total hits, walks, and outs, your rows should contain the hits, walks, and outs for each game. Your third dimension should indicate the game. Display the values for each player who played by game. Do not display any data for a game in which a player did not participate. Display the total number of hits, walks, and outs by game and by season.

The user instructions should be the same as in Exercise 1. Following is a copy of the output that should appear when running your program with the test data from Exercise 1.

Player	Hits	Walks	Outs
1	2	2	2
2	0	0	6
3	2	1	3
4	1	2	3

7	0	0	3
8	1	4	1
9	3	2	1
18	4	2	0
20	0	5	1
Game 1			
Totals	13	18	20
2	0	5	1
3	1	2	3
4	2	1	3
7	0	0	3
10	2	2	2
11	6	0	0
12	2	2	2
17	4	2	0
20	0	0	6
Game 2			
Totals	17	14	20
1	2	2	2
2	0	0	6
8	1	4	1
9	3	2	1
11	6	0	0
13	2	1	3
16	2	2	2
18	4	2	0
20	0	5	1
Game 3			
Totals	20	18	16
2	0	5	1
3	1	4	1
4	2	2	2
5	2	2	2
6	6	0	0
7	3	2	1
14	1	2	3
17	0	0	3
20	0	0	6
Game 4			
Totals	15	17	19
3	2	1	3
8	4	2	0
11	2	2	2
13	6	0	0
14	1	2	3
15	0	0	1
17	0	0	3
18	1	4	1
19	3	2	1
Game 5			
Totals	19	13	14
Season			
Totals	83	80	89

1. b.   Write a Java program based on the design that you created in Exercise 2a. Save the program as **Basebal4.java** in the Chap09 folder on your Student Disk, and then compile, run, and test the program. Copy the instructions, input, and output that are displayed, and paste them in a block comment at the end of your program. Then print your program to submit with your work.

APPLICATIONS OF ARRAYS AND STRINGS

In this chapter, you will:

♦ Learn how to implement the sequential search algorithm

♦ Explore how to sort an array using the selection sort algorithm

♦ Learn how to implement the binary search algorithm

♦ Become aware of the class Vector

♦ Learn about manipulating strings using the class String

CHAPTER 10: ASSIGNMENT COVER SHEET

Name _____   Date _____

Section _____

Lab Assignments	Grade
Lab 10.1 Implementing the Sequential Search Algorithm	
Lab 10.2 Sorting an Array Using Selection Sort	
Lab 10.3 Implementing the Binary Search Algorithm	
Lab 10.4 Using the class Vector (Critical Thinking Exercise)	
Lab 10.5 Using String Methods (Critical Thinking Exercise)	
Total Grade	

See your instructor or the introduction to this book for instructions on submitting your assignments.

LAB 10.1 IMPLEMENTING THE SEQUENTIAL SEARCH ALGORITHM

Lists can be stored in arrays. You can perform the following basic operations on a list:

- Input a list.

- Output a list.

- Search the list for a given item.

- Sort the list.

- Insert an item in the list.

- Delete an item from the list.

One way to search a list is to determine the length of the list and the item for which you are searching. After searching a list, you need to know if the item was found. If the item was found, you need to know the location or a reference to the element where it was found.

Searching each location of a list until an item is found is called a sequential search or linear search.

Objectives

In this lab, you search a list of a particular size for a value, and then indicate whether the item is found. If it is, you indicate the location where the item was found.

After completing this lab, you will be able to:

- Search a list of a given size for a particular value.

- Report if an item is found in the list.

- If the item was found, report the location in the list where it was found.

Estimated completion time: **50–60 minutes**

Implementing the Sequential Search Algorithm

In the following exercises, you design and write a program that searches a list for a number and reports where it is found.

1. a. Design a program that simulates a contest for a radio station that awards a $10,000 prize to the first caller who correctly guesses a number in a list of randomly generated numbers. A caller can make one guess. The contest is held until a number has been matched or the user enters a value of -1. The following numbers were found using a program to randomly generate 20 numbers. Either assign the following twenty different values between 1 and 500 to an array, or write your own program to randomly generate your numbers.

```
42
468
335
1
170
225
479
359
463
465
206
146
```

```
282
329
462
492
496
443
328
437
```

Display a message indicating the winning number, the location in the list of numbers, the number of calls made, and the amount of the prize.

Following is a copy of some of the screen results that might appear after running your program, depending on the data entered.

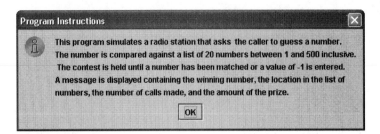

Figure 10-1   Program Instructions dialog box

If the program finds a value on the list with the first guess, the following dialog boxes appear depending on the data entered:

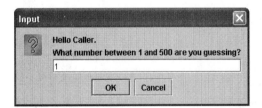

Figure 10-2   Caller Guess Input dialog box

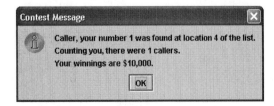

Figure 10-3   Contest Message dialog box

If the user does not immediately enter a value on the list when the program runs, the following additional dialog boxes should appear depending on the data entered:

Figure 10-4   Guess Not Found Message dialog box

Figure 10-5   Invalid Guess Message dialog box

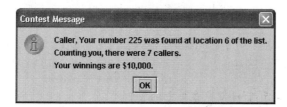

Figure 10-6   Guess Message dialog box

Write your design in the following space. Your design should be a list describing what happens at each line in the program, or should use the format your instructor requires.

1. b. Write a Java program based on the design that you created in Exercise 1a. Save the program as
        Prize.java in the Chap10 folder on your Student Disk, and then compile, run, and test the
        program. Either copy the dialog boxes that appear and paste them into a document or print
        screens of the dialog boxes. Then print your program to submit with your work.

LAB 10.2 SORTING AN ARRAY USING SELECTION SORT

The selection sort algorithm rearranges a list by selecting an element in the list and moving it to its proper position. For example, first the smallest item in the list is moved to the first location. Starting with the second item in the list, the next smallest item is then moved to the second location. You can also sort by placing the largest value in the first position, the second largest value in the second position, and so on.

Once a list has been sorted—also called ordered—the list can be sequentially searched. In a sequential search on an ordered list, once a value in the list is greater than the value being searched for, the search is complete and the item is not found. (In a descending list, once a value in the list is smaller than the value being searched for, the search is complete and the item is not found.)

Objectives

In this lab, you become acquainted with the selection sort. You also search an ordered list of a particular size for a value. Indicate whether the item is found; if it is, indicate the location where the item was found. If the number is not in the search list, discontinue the search once a list value exceeds the search value.

After completing this lab, you will be able to:

- Sort an unordered list using the selection sort.

- Search an ordered list of a given size for a particular value.

- Report if an item is found in the list.

- If the item was found, report the location in the list where it was found.

- If the item was not found, stop the search once a list value exceeds the search value and then indicate that the value was not found.

Estimated completion time: **60–90 minutes**

Sorting an Array Using Selection Sort

In the following exercises, you design and write a program that sorts a list.

1. a.   Design a program that sorts the same list of values that you used in Lab 10.1. Your design should be a list of method calls where all work is performed within a method. Sort the array using the selection sort algorithm. Write the array to an output file called **prizeNos.srt** and save it in your Chap10 folder on your Student Disk. Output the original list and the sorted list to the screen. Print the **prizeNos.srt** file and compare the lists.

   Following is a copy of the screen results that might appear after running your program, depending on the data entered. Your beginning list:

   ```
   42
   468
   335
   1
   170
   225
   479
   359
   463
   ```

```
465
206
146
282
329
462
492
496
443
328
437
```

Your sorted list:

```
1
42
146
170
206
225
282
328
329
335
359
437
443
462
463
465
468
479
492
496
```

The following list is the file **prizeNos.srt**:

```
1
42
146
170
206
225
282
328
329
335
359
437
443
462
463
465
468
479
492
496
```

Write your design in the following space. Your design should be a list describing what happens at each line in the program, or should use the format your instructor requires.

1. b.   Write a Java program based on the design that you created in Exercise 1a. Save the program as **SortList.java** in the Chap10 folder on your Student Disk, and then compile, run, and test the program. Copy the instructions, input, and output that are displayed, and paste them in a block comment at the end of your program. Then print your program to submit with your work.

2. a.   Write a program design to sequentially search the ordered list **prizeNos.srt** created in Exercise 1. Because the list is ordered, you can make your search a "smart search" by first checking if the value is less than or greater than the first element in the list. If the value falls in the range of the list, then the list should be searched. You can start searching at the beginning or at the end of the list. Include an output line that shows how many comparisons it takes to search for each guess.

You should have the same screen results as those in Lab 10.1. You will also have additional output messages depending on the data entered.

If the guess is less than the smallest number on the list or greater than the largest number of the list, the following message should be displayed:

```
It took 0 comparisons to check the list.
```

For all other guesses, the program will display the following message:

```
It took n comparisons to check the list.
```

In this message, n is a value between 1 and 20 inclusively.

Write your design in the following space. Your design should be a list describing what happens at each line in the program, or should use the format your instructor requires.

2. b. Implement the new design in Java. Save the program as **Prize2.java** in the Chap10 folder on your Student Disk. After executing your program, select and copy everything that appears on your screen. Paste the copied text into a comment block at the end of your program.

Lab 10.3 Implementing the Binary Search Algorithm

A sequential search on an ordered list usually requires searching about half the list. For long lists, the binary search is much faster than the sequential search. The first search item is compared to the middle element of the list. Then the search item is compared to either the middle of the first half of the list or the middle of the second half of the list. This process is repeated until the search item is found or there are no more list items.

Each time the item is searched, the list is cut in half. Because every iteration of the loop makes two item comparisons, the binary search will make at most $2 * \log_2 n + 2$ item comparisons. In nonmathematical terms, the number of comparisons can be calculated by the size of the list. This example has a list size of 20. The number 2 raised to the power of 4 is 16. The number 2 raised to the power of 5 is 32. The list size of 20 is greater than 2 to the power of 4 and less than 2 to the power of 5. It should take four or five comparisons to search the list because the list is cut in half each time.

Objectives

In this lab, you use a binary search on an ordered list of a given size to find a particular value. Indicate whether the item is found. If it is, indicate the location where the item was found.

After completing this lab, you will be able to:

- Use a binary search on an ordered list of a given size for a particular value.

- Report if an item is found in the ordered list.

- If the item was found, report the location in the list where it was found.

Estimated completion time: **40–50 minutes**

Implementing the Binary Search Algorithm

In the following exercises, you revise the radio caller program you created in Lab 10.2 to use a binary search algorithm.

1. a.   Continue working with the program that determines the winning caller to a radio show by revising the program you created in Lab 10.2 to determine which caller number wins the prize and the amount of the prize awarded. Use the binary search algorithm and the **prizeNos.srt** file you created in Lab 10.2.

Make your search a "smart search" by first checking to see whether the value is less than or greater than the first element in the list. If the value falls in the range of the list, then the list should be searched. Include an output line that shows how many comparisons it takes to search for each guess.

You should have the same screen results as those in Lab 10.1. An additional output message also appears, depending on the data entered. If the guess is less than the smallest number or greater than the largest number on the list, the following message should be displayed:

```
It took 0 comparisons to check the list.
```

All other guesses will display one of the following messages:

```
It took 4 comparisons to check the list.
```

or

```
It took 5 comparisons to check the list.
```

Write your design in the following space. Your design should be a list describing what happens at each line in the program, or should use the format your instructor requires.

1. b. Implement the new design in Java. Save the program as **Prize3.java** in the Chap10 folder on your Student Disk. After executing your program, select and copy everything that appears on your screen. Paste the copied text into a comment block at the end of your program.

LAB 10.4 USING THE CLASS VECTOR

One of the limitations of arrays discussed so far is that once you create an array, its size remains fixed. Also, inserting or removing an element in the array at a specific position might require the program to shift the elements of the array.

In addition to arrays, Java provides the class Vector to implement a list. A Vector object can grow and shrink during program execution. Every element of a Vector object is a reference variable of the type Object that stores the address of any object. You can store the address of the object holding the data into a Vector object element. Values of primitive data types cannot be directly assigned to a Vector element.

The class Vector contains various methods for manipulation. The class Vector is contained in the package java.util. Values of primitive data types cannot be directly assigned to a Vector element. You must first wrap the primitive data type element into an appropriate wrapper class.

Objectives

In this lab, you become acquainted with the class Vector and various members of the class Vector to create a list in sorted order.

After completing this lab, you will be able to:

- Create Vector objects or the Vector class.

- Use various members of the class Vector

- Wrap a primitive data type element into an appropriate wrapper to be used as a Vector object.

Estimated completion time: **50–60 minutes**

Using the class Vector

In the following exercises, you design and write a program using the class Vector.

1. a. *Critical Thinking Exercise*: Design a program to read values from a file into a Vector in sorted order. Create a file named **Numbers.txt** with the 20 unsorted values that you used in Lab 10.1. Once all values have been entered, display the contents of the vector to the screen.

    Following is a copy of the screen results that might appear after running your program, depending on the data entered. Your unsorted values:

    42
    468
    335
    1
    170
    225
    479
    359
    463
    465
    206
    146
    282
    329
    462
    492
    496
    443

```
328
437
```

Your sorted vector:

```
1
42
146
170
206
225
282
328
329
335
359
437
443
462
463
465
468
```

Write your design in the following space. Your design should be a list describing what happens at each line in the program, or should use the format your instructor requires.

1. b.   Save the program as **BldList.java** in the Chap10 folder on your Student Disk. After executing your program, select and copy everything that appears on your screen. Paste the copied text into a comment block at the end of your program.

LAB 10.5 USING STRING METHODS

Java provides various string methods to manipulate individual characters of a string as well as substrings of the string. The class String is contained in the package java.lang.

Objectives

In this lab, you use string methods to search a string for the occurrence of a substring and replace with another substring.

After completing this lab, you will be able to:

- Search a string for the occurrence of a substring.

- Replace a substring in a string with another substring.

- Change uppercase and lowercase characters to match the uppercase and lowercase use of the substring.

Estimated completion time: 50–60 minutes

Using String Methods

In the following exercises, you design and write programs that use string methods.

1. a. *Critical Thinking Exercise*: In this exercise, you design a search and replace program for a word processor. Ask the user to enter a string, a substring to search in the string, and a substring to replace the search substring. Disregard the cases of the substrings. Use the case of the original string in the newly created string.

   Following is a copy of the screen results that might appear after running your program, depending on the data entered. The input entered by the user is shown in bold.

   ```
   This program simulates the search and replace feature of a word
   processor.
   The user enters a sentence, a substring to search,
   and a substring to use for substitution.

   Please enter the string.
   Your teacher will assign a "Teach the Teacher" project for you to
   teach.

   Please enter the search string.
   teach

   Please enter the replacement string.
   instruct

   Your new sentence is:
   Your instructor will assign an "Instruct the Instructor" project for
   you to instruct.
   ```

Write your design in the following space. Your design should be a list describing what happens at each line in the program, or should use the format your instructor requires.

1. b. Save the program as **Search.java** in the Chap10 folder on your Student Disk. After executing your program, select and copy everything that appears on your screen. Paste the copied text into a comment block at the end of your program.

INHERITANCE AND COMPOSITION

In this chapter, you will:

♦ Learn about inheritance

♦ Learn about `subclasses` and `superclasses`

♦ Explore how to override the methods of a superclass

♦ Learn how constructors of superclasses and subclasses work

♦ Learn how to construct the header file of a subclass

♦ Learn about composition

♦ Examine abstract classes

♦ Become aware of interfaces

Chapter 11: Assignment Cover Sheet

Name _____   Date _____

Section _____

Lab Assignments	Grade
Lab 11.1 Overriding Member Methods of the superclass and Using Constructors of subclasses and superclasses	
Lab 11.2 Using Protected Members of the superclass and Relating Classes through Composition (Critical Thinking Exercise)	
Lab 11.3 Designing and Writing an Application Program Using Inheritance (Critical Thinking Exercise)	
Lab 11.4 Differentiating public, private, and protected members of a superclass	
Total Grade	

See your instructor or the introduction to this book for instructions on submitting your assignments.

LAB 11.1 OVERRIDING MEMBER METHODS OF THE SUPERCLASS AND USING CONSTRUCTORS OF SUBCLASSES AND SUPERCLASSES

You can create new classes from existing classes. You do not need to change the existing class directly; instead, you can inherit members of a class when designing another class. Inheritance is the characteristic that lets you create classes from existing classes. The new classes are called subclasses, and the existing classes are called superclasses.

Each subclass can be a superclass for a future subclass. In single inheritance, the subclass is derived from a single superclass; in multiple inheritance, the subclass is derived from more than one superclass. Java supports single inheritance, that is, a Java class can extend the definition of only one class. The general syntax of deriving a class from an existing class follows:

```
modifier(s) class ClassName extends ExistingClassName modifiers(s)
{
memberList
}
```

The private members of the superclass are private members of the subclass, which means that the members of the subclass cannot directly access them. The subclass can override, or redefine, the public member methods of the superclass. The redefinition applies only to the objects of the subclass.

A subclass can have its own constructor. The constructors of the subclass can directly initialize only the instance variables of the subclass. When a subclass object is instantiated, the subclass object must also automatically execute one of the constructors of the superclass to initialize the (private) instance variables. A call to a constructor of the superclass is specified in the definition of a subclass constructor by using the reserved word `super`.

Objectives

In this lab, you define subclasses by extending superclasses.

After completing this lab exercise, you will be able to:

- Write a subclass by extending the superclass.

- Create instance variables of the subclass and the superclass.

- Recognize the difference between instance variables of the subclass and instance variables of the superclass.

- Use a constructor of a subclass to access the constructor of the superclass.

Estimated completion time: **120–150 minutes**

Overriding Member Methods of the superclass and Using Constructors of subclasses and superclasses

In the following exercises, you examine a UML diagram, and then design and create a Java program based on this diagram.

1. a.   Following is a UML diagram for the class DateRec.

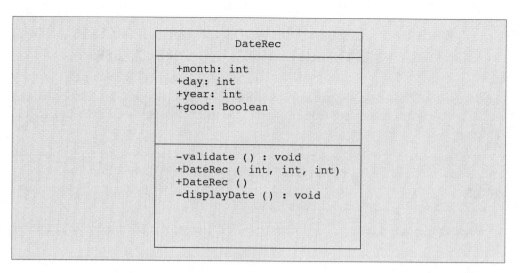

Figure 11-1 UML diagram of the class DateRec

Create a DateRec class using the UML diagram shown in Figure 11-1 to write a Java class. The DateRec class should include the following elements:

- Design a default DateRec() constructor that assigns the values of 1, 1, and 2006 to the appropriate instance variables of the object. Also set the Boolean variable good to true in the default constructor.

- Design a DateRec() constructor with parameters to accept values for month, day, and year through the parameter list.

- Call the validate() method to verify those values.

- Design the validate() method to verify that the month, day, and year are within proper ranges and assign true or false to the instance variable good of the object if the values are valid.

- Design the method displayDate() to display the values for month, day, and year.

Write your class design in the following space. Your design should be a list describing what happens at each line in the program, or should use the format your instructor requires.

1. b. Write your class and name it **DateRec.java**. Save the program in the folder you created for classes on your hard disk (or the location specified by your instructor). If you are using the folders specified in Chapter 6, save the program in a folder named jpfpatpd/ch11/Ch11ClassDef.

Compile your class to be used later. (You cannot run your class code because you have not written a program to test the operations of the class DateRec.)

1. c. Design a program with a main method to test the DateRec class. The program should:

- Include all comments for documentation and identification of the program in your design.
- Create an object named today of the type DateRec using the current date for month, day, and year.
- Create an object anyDay of the type DateRec with no arguments.
- Create an object noDay with invalid date values.
- Call the displayDate() method to output the values after they have been assigned.

Following is a copy of the screen results that might appear after running your program, depending on the data entered.

```
13/1/2004
You entered an invalid date

11/2/2006
1/1/2006
13/1/2004
```

Write your design in the following space. Your design should be a list describing what happens at each line in the program, or should use the format your instructor requires.

1. d. Write a Java program based on the design that you created in Exercise 1c. For readability, insert blank lines to separate parts of the program. Include comments to explain the different sections of code.

Save the program as **DateTst.java** in the Chap11 folder on your Student Disk. Compile, execute, and test the program.

2. a. Use the UML diagram example in Figure 11-1 as a guide to create a UML diagram for a class named Animal to:

- Include private integer values named lifeExpectancy and weight.
- Include a character value named gender and a string value called name.
- Allow for a public string value called type.
- Design an Animal() constructor with parameters to accept values for each data member.
- Include a public void method named printValues() with no parameters in the Animal class.
- Design the printValues() method that will display all data members for the object of that class.

Create your UML diagram in the following space.

2. b. Write a Java class based on the UML diagram for Animal that you designed in Exercise 2a. Create the class in the following space.

2. c. Enter your class and name it **Animal.java**. Save the program in the folder you created for classes on your hard disk (or the location specified by your instructor). If you are using the folders specified in Chapter 6, save the program in a folder named jpfpatpd/ch11/Ch11ClassDef.

Compile your class to be used later.

2. d. Design a program with a main method to test the Animal class. Your program should:

- Include all comments for documentation and identification of the program in your design.

- Create an object named elephant of the type Animal. For gender, use 'm' for male, 'f' for female, 'n' for a neutered male, and 's' for a spayed female. You can expect a male elephant to live 65 years and weigh around 7 tons (14,000 pounds).

- Using these facts, assign values to each data member in the class and call the printValues() method to output the values after they have been assigned.

Following is a copy of the screen results that might appear after running your program, depending on the data entered.

```
A male elephant named Jumbo should live to be 65 and weigh 14000 pounds.
```

Write your design in the following space. Your design should be a list describing what happens at each line in the program, or should use the format your instructor requires.

2. e.   Write a Java program based on the design that you created in Exercise 2d. For readability, insert blank lines to separate parts of the program. Include comments to explain the different sections of code.

Save the program as **AnimlTst.java** in the Chap11 folder on your Student Disk. Compile, execute, and test the program.

3. a.   Create a UML diagram for the subclass named Pet that extends the class Animal. Include the following elements in the program:

- Include a string value named home and a Boolean value named bites as private members.

- Include a Pet() constructor with parameters to initialize all data members of the class and to call the Animal() constructor.

- Allow a void method named printValues() with no parameters.

- Include the printValues() method that will display all data members for the object of that class and then call the printValues() method of the Animal class when necessary to display private data members of the superclass.

Create your UML diagram in the following space.

3. b.   Use the UML diagram for Pet to write a Java class that you designed in Exercise 3a. Create the class in the following space.

3. c.   Enter your class and name it **Pet.java**. Save the program in the folder you created for classes on your hard disk (or the location specified by your instructor). If you are using the folders specified in Chapter 6, save the program in a folder named jpfpatpd/ch11/Ch11ClassDef.

Compile your class to be used later.

3. d.   Design a program with a main method to test the Pet class. Your program should:

- Include all comments for documentation and identification of the program in your design.

- Create an object named dog of the type Pet. You can expect a spayed dog to live 11 years, and weigh around 20 pounds. Your dog should live indoors and not bite.

- Using these facts, assign values to each data member in the class and call the printValues() method to output the values after they have been assigned.

Following is a copy of the screen results that might appear after running your program, depending on the data entered.

```
A spayed dog named Fifi should live to be 11 and weigh 20 pounds.

Your dog lives indoors and does not bite.
```

Write your design in the following space. Your design should be a list describing what happens at each line in the program, or should use the format your instructor requires.

Save the program as **PetTst.java** in the Chap11 folder on your Student Disk. Compile, execute, and test the program.

LAB 11.2 ACCESSING PROTECTED MEMBERS OF THE SUPERCLASS

The members of a class are classified into three categories: public, private, and protected. For a superclass to give access to a member of its subclass while preventing direct access outside the class, you must declare that member using the modifier **protected**. A subclass can directly access the protected member of a superclass.

Composition is another way to relate two classes. In composition, one or more members of a class are objects of another class type.

Objectives

In this lab, you access protected members of the superclass from its subclass and write a subclass that uses composition.

After completing this lab, you will be able to:

■ Access protected members of the superclass from its subclass.

■ Use composition in a subclass.

Estimated completion time: **60–90 minutes**

Accessing Protected Members of the superclass

In the following exercises, you revise a UML diagram, class design, and code to access protected members of a superclass.

1. Change your UML diagram, class design, and code for the Animal class to make the data member name public and the remaining data members protected instead of private. Also write a default Animal2 constructor containing no instructions. Save your changed class as Animal2, revise your code to reflect that change, and recompile your class. Change your class design and code for your **AnimlTst.java** program to test the Animal2 class. Save your changed program as **AnimlT2.java**, and then recompile and run the program. Compare the results from **AnimlTst.java** and **AnimlT2.java**. They should be the same.

2. a. *Critical Thinking Exercise:* Write a UML diagram for the subclass named VetPatient that extends the class Animal2. Include the following elements in the program:

■ Contain as private members DateRec members named dateIn and dateOut, a double member named charges, and a string member named procedure.

■ Include instance variables of the DateRec class.

■ Include a VetPatient() constructor with parameters to initialize all data members of the class and to call the Animal() constructor.

■ Allow a void method named printValues() with no parameters. Design the printValues() method that will display all data members for the object of that class and then call the printValues() method of the Animal class when necessary to display private data members of the superclass.

■ Format money amounts to show two decimal places.

Create your UML diagram in the following space.

2. b.   Use the UML diagram for VetPatient to write a Java class that you designed in Exercise 2a. Create the class in the following space.

2. c.   Enter your class and name it **VetPatient.java**. Save the program in the folder you created for classes on your hard disk (or the location specified by your instructor). If you are using the folders specified in Chapter 6, save the program in a folder named jpfpatpd/ch11/Ch11ClassDef.

Compile your class to be used later.

2. d.   Design a program with a main method to test the VetPatient class. Your program should:

- Include all comments for documentation and identification of the program in your design.

- Create an object named horse of the type VetPatient. You can expect a spayed racehorse to live 25 years, weigh around 1,000 pounds, and have regular exams by a veterinarian.

- Using these facts, assign values to each data member in the class and call the printValues() method to output the values after they have been assigned.

Following is a copy of the screen results that might appear after running your program, depending on the data entered.

```
A spayed horse named Pretty Filly should live to be 25 and weigh
1000 pounds.

The horse checked in 8/30/2006 and checked out 8/31/2006.
The procedure performed was a check-up at a cost of $58.00.
```

Write your design in the following space. Your design should be a list describing what happens at each line in the program, or should use the format your instructor requires.

2. e.   Write a Java program based on the design that you created in Exercise 2d. For readability, insert blank lines to separate parts of the program. Include comments to explain the different sections of code.

Save the program as **VetTst.java** in the Chap11 folder on your Student Disk. Compile, execute, and test the program.

LAB 11.3 DESIGNING AND WRITING AN APPLICATION PROGRAM USING INHERITANCE

One advantage of using inheritance is the ability to use code that has been tested for accuracy. This requires the program to test the class so that it can be reused. Test programs should access each data member and method of the class. Once the class is tested, you can write a subclass that extends the superclass.

Objectives

In this lab, you design and write a subclass extending the Animal2 class and an application program that uses the subclass.

After completing this lab, you will be able to:

- Design a subclass extending a superclass to perform a particular purpose.

- Design and write an application program with a user-defined subclass.

Estimated completion time: **60–90 minutes**

Designing and Writing an Application Program Using Inheritance

In the following exercises, you create a UML diagram, and design and write a Java program that uses inheritance.

1. a. *Critical Thinking Exercise*: Create a UML diagram for the class named VetOffice that extends the superclass Animal2. The subclass VetOffice will be used by an application program you are to write for a veterinary practice.

   The class VetOffice should contain the following elements:

   - public data members double charges and int procedure

   - private data members int days, String type, char gender

   - a void method initialize() that has a parameter integer array costs

   - a public void method printValues() that has parameters DateRec today and a String array messages

   The method initialize() is used to perform the following tasks:

   - Prompt the user for the number corresponding to service desired until a valid service is entered.

   - If a user enters selection 15 (other), prompt the user for the cost of the procedure.

   - Prompt the user for the name of the pet.

   - Ask the user if the pet is a cat or dog. If another pet type is entered, display a message stating that the practice is limited to dogs and cats.

   - Prompt the user for the gender of the pet until a valid gender is entered.

   - When the boarding service is chosen, prompt the user for the number of days the patient is to board.

   - Display a message showing the service performed, the gender, species, and name of the pet, the date of service, the procedure number, the procedure description, and the cost of service.

The method printValues() is used to display a message showing the service performed, the gender, species, and name of the pet, the date of service, the procedure number, the procedure description, and the cost of service.

Create your UML diagram in the following space.

1. b.   Use the UML diagram for VetOffice to write a Java class that you designed in Exercise 1a. Create the class in the following space.

1. c. Enter your class and name it **VetOffice.java**. Save the program in the folder you created for classes on your hard disk (or the location specified by your instructor). If you are using the folders specified in Chapter 6, save the program in a folder named jpfpatpd/ch11/Ch11ClassDef.

Compile your class to be used later.

1. d. Design an application program named VetBooks. Include all comments for documentation and identification of the program in your design. Your program should:

- Prompt the user for today's date.

- Display the instructions to use the program and then repeat instructions when requested.

- Create a daily output report file named **patients.txt** with the day's procedures.

- Produce a daily output report that includes a title with the clinic name, today's date, and column headings for patient, service, and fees.

- Calculate the total daily fees and output the total to the daily output report.

- Limit each patient to a single procedure, if necessary.

Following is a copy of the screen results that might appear after running your program, depending on the data entered. The user is first prompted for today's date.

```
Healthy Pet Clinic Daily Transactions
Please enter today's date separated by spaces (mm dd yyyy):
12 02 2005
```

The instructions should resemble the following:

```
The Healthy Pet Clinic offers services for your cats and dogs.
 1  Anesthesia                  $40
 2  Annual cat inoculations     $75
 3  Annual dog inoculations     $60
 4  Boarding per night          $18
 5  Check-ups                   $40
 6  Declawing                   $75
 7  Dog grooming                $75
 8  Nail or claw clipping       $8
 9  Neutering                   $50
10  Spaying                     $75
11  Worming                     $10
12  Surgery type 1              $100
13  Surgery type 2              $200
14  Surgery type 3              $300
15  Other
 0  Quit
```

The following prompts should appear until the user enters a 0 to end the program or until a valid procedure number has been entered.

```
Please enter the number of the service that you wish: 2
Please enter the name of your pet: Ferdinand
Please enter whether your pet is a cat or a dog: cat
Please enter the gender of your pet (m)ale, (f)emale, (s)payed,
(n)eutered: n
Would you like to see the instructions (y)es or (n)o: n
```

If an invalid number of service is entered, the following message and prompt should be displayed until a valid procedure number is entered.

```
You entered an invalid procedure.
Please enter the number of the service that you wish: 2
```

If a 15 is entered as the procedure number, the following prompt should appear.

```
Please enter the cost of this procedure: 85
```

If an invalid pet type is entered, the following message and prompt should be displayed until a valid pet type is entered.

```
This practice is limited to dogs and cats.
Please enter whether your pet is a cat or a dog: cat
```

If an invalid gender type is entered, the following message and prompt should be displayed until a valid gender type is entered.

```
You did not enter a valid gender.
Please enter the gender of your pet (m)ale, (f)emale, (s)payed,
(n)eutered: n
```

If procedure 4 (boarding per night $18) is chosen, the following prompt should appear.

```
How many days do you wish to board? 1
```

If a positive number is not entered, the following message and prompt should be displayed until a positive number is entered.

```
You entered an invalid number of days.
```

For each patient that comes in, a message similar to the following one should appear, depending on the input data.

```
The following services were performed on your neutered cat Ferdinand:
12/2/2005        2  Annual cat inoculations      at a cost of $75.00.
```

The output file **patients.txt** should resemble the following report, depending on the data entered.

```
         The Healthy Pet Clinic Services for 12-2-2005

      Patient                    Service                    Fees

   Bowser             1  Anesthesia                      $  40.00
   Ferdinand          2  Annual cat inoculations         $  75.00
   Fifi               3  Annual dog inoculations         $  60.00
   Rover              4  Boarding per night              $  54.00
   Harvard            5  Check-ups                       $  40.00
   Sweetie            6  Declawing                       $  75.00
   Isabel             7  Dog grooming                    $  75.00
   Tia                8  Nail or claw clipping           $   8.00
   Spot               9  Neutering                       $  50.00
   Fluffy            10  Spaying                         $  75.00
   Gretchen          11  Worming                         $  10.00
   Heinrich          12  Surgery type 1                  $100.00
   Lucky             13  Surgery type 2                  $200.00
   Zachery           14  Surgery type 3                  $300.00
   Fido              15  Other                           $  20.00


   Total                                                 $1182.00
```

Write your design in the following space. Your design should be a list describing what happens at each line in the program, or should use the format your instructor requires.

1. e. Write a Java program based on the design that you created in Exercise 1d. For readability, insert blank lines to separate parts of the program. Include comments to explain the different sections of code. Save the program as **VetBooks.java** in the Chap11 folder on your Student Disk. Compile, run, and test the program with input that tests all cases. Copy the instructions, input, and output that are displayed, and paste them in a block comment at the end of your program.

LAB 11.4 DIFFERENTIATING PUBLIC, PRIVATE, AND PROTECTED MEMBERS OF A SUPERCLASS

A protected member of a superclass is public to the subclass, but private outside of the subclass and the superclass. By using the `protected` specifier, you can create a class member that can be inherited and accessed but remain private otherwise.

Objectives

In this lab, you become acquainted with the differences among public, private, and protected specifiers for accessing members of a superclass. You also learn about the inheritance of these specifiers.

After completing this lab, you will be able to:

- Differentiate public, private, and protected specifiers of members of a class.

Estimated completion time: **20-30 minutes**

Differentiating public, private, and protected Members of a superclass

The following exercises are designed to demonstrate your understanding of the differences among public, private, and protected specifiers of members of a class so that you are better prepared to design and write programs that use protected members of a class in inheritance.

1. Show by example how a subclass inherits a superclass.

2. What members of the superclass are included in the subclass?

3. Can a subclass inherit public members of the superclass as private members of the subclass?

4. If so, how are these members accessed in the subclass?

5. Can a subclass inherit private members of the superclass as public members of the subclass?

6. How are these members accessed in the subclass?

7. Can a subclass inherit protected members of the superclass as public members of the subclass?

8. How are these members accessed in the subclass?

9. Can a subclass inherit public members of the superclass as protected members of the subclass?

10. Can a subclass inherit protected members of the superclass as private members of the subclass?

EXCEPTIONS AND EVENT HANDLING

In this chapter, you will:

♦ Learn what an exception is

♦ Become aware of the hierarchy of exception classes

♦ Learn about checked and unchecked exceptions

♦ Learn how to handle exceptions within a program

♦ See how a try/catch block is used to handle exceptions

♦ Discover how to throw and rethrow an exception

♦ Learn how to handle events in a program

CHAPTER 12: ASSIGNMENT COVER SHEET

Name _____   Date _____

Section _____

Lab Assignments	Grade
Lab 12.1 Catching Exceptions and Processing Exceptions During Program Execution using try and catch Blocks (Critical Thinking Exercise)	
Lab 12.2 Combining catch Blocks using the Operator instanceof	
Lab 12.3 Using Exception Handling Techniques (Critical Thinking Exercise)	
Lab 12.4 Creating Your Own Exception Classes	
Lab 12.5 Using Event Handling (Critical Thinking Exercise)	
Total Grade	

See your instructor or the introduction to this book for instructions on submitting your assignments.

LAB 12.1 CATCHING EXCEPTIONS AND PROCESSING EXCEPTIONS DURING PROGRAM EXECUTION USING TRY AND CATCH BLOCKS

Until now your programs have not included code to handle exceptions. If exceptions occurred during program execution, the program terminated with an appropriate error message. However, with some exceptions, you don't want the program to simply ignore the exception and terminate.

One common way to provide exception-handling code is to add such code at the point where an error might occur. Java provides a number of exception classes. The class Throwable, which is derived from the class Object, is the superclass of the class Exception and contains various constructors and methods. Some methods getMessage, printStackTrace, and toString are public and so are inherited by the subclasses of the class Throwable.

Java's predefined exceptions are divided into two categories—checked exceptions and unchecked exceptions. Any exception that can be analyzed by the compiler is called a checked exception. For example, IOExceptions are checked exceptions. Enabling the compiler to check for these types of exceptions reduces the number of exceptions not properly handled by the program. The throws clause lists the types of exceptions thrown by the method. The syntax of the throws clause is:

```
throws ExceptionType1, ExceptionType2, ...
```

where ExceptionType1, ExceptionType2, and so on are the names of the exception classes.

Exceptions such as division by zero or index out of bounds may not be capable to determine at compilation. These types of exceptions are called unchecked exceptions. These exceptions belong to a subclass of the class RuntimeException.

Statements that might generate an exception are placed in a `try` block. The `try` block also contains statements that should not be executed if an exception occurs. The `try` block is followed by zero or more `catch` blocks. A `catch` block specifies the type of exception it can catch and contains an exception handler. The last `catch` block may or may not be followed by a `finally` block. Any code contained in a `finally` block always executes, regardless of whether an exception occurs. If a `try` block has no `catch` block, then it must have the `finally` block.

Objectives

In this lab, you catch exceptions that should be caught and process them during program execution.

After completing this lab exercise, you will be able to:

- Catch exceptions that should be caught.

- Process caught exceptions during program execution.

- Use multiple catch blocks for multiple exceptions of different types in the same program.

Estimated completion time: **90–120 minutes**

Catching Exceptions and Processing Exceptions During Program Execution using try and catch Blocks

In the following exercises, you revise a program to catch and process exceptions.

1. a.   *Critical Thinking Exercise*: In Chapter 11, you wrote a program called VetBooks that writes a daily report to a file. Redesign the VetBooks program to meet the following criteria:

    - If your output file is written to the hard disk, change the path to write your output file to either your floppy disk or Zip disk.

- Place your `try` and `catch` blocks in a loop that continues until the user selects the option to quit.

- Use a `catch` block for the FileNotFoundException exception. Allow the user to insert a disk and continue the program.

- Use a `catch` block for the NoSuchElementException exception. Allow the user to continue the program when data is not entered.

- Use a `catch` block for the NumberFormatException exception. Allow the user to re-enter the data in the proper format.

- Create Boolean values to keep track of whether the file has already been opened after an exception has been thrown and whether the date has already been entered.

- Test to see if the date is valid (the class DateRec has a public Boolean member good that indicates if the date falls within a valid date range).

Following is a copy of the screen results that might appear while running your program when a disk is not inserted.

```
Unable to open file, please insert disk.
Press Enter to continue.
```

Following is a copy of the screen results that might appear if three integer values are not entered for the date.

```
You did not enter any data.
```

Following is a copy of the screen results that might appear if the date is entered with character data.

```
Your data was not in the correct format.
```

Once your disk is inserted, and the date is entered correctly, your output should match the same output as your VetBooks program, depending on the data entered.

Write your design in the following space. Your design should be a list describing what happens at each line in the program, or should use the format your instructor requires.

1. b. Write a Java program based on the design you created in Exercise 1a. Save the program as **VBooksEx.java** in the Chap12 folder on your Student Disk. Compile, execute, and test the program. Copy the instructions, input, and output that are displayed, and paste them in a block comment at the end of your program. Then print your program to submit with your work.

LAB 12.2 COMBINING CATCH BLOCKS USING THE OPERATOR INSTANCEOF

You can use the instanceof operator to determine if a reference variable points to an object of a particular class. You can combine multiple catch blocks into a single catch block and then use the instanceof operator to determine which exception was thrown.

Objectives

In this lab, you combine multiple catch blocks into one catch block and use the operator instanceof to determine which exception was thrown.

After completing this lab, you will be able to:

- Combine multiple catch blocks into one catch block.

- Use the operator instanceof to determine which exception was thrown.

Estimated completion time: **20–30 minutes**

Combining catch Blocks using the Operator instanceof

In the following exercises, you design and write a program using the instanceof operator.

1. a.   Change your class design for your **VBooksEx** program to combine your three catch blocks in one catch block. Use the instanceof operator to determine which exception was thrown. Your output should match the same output as your **VBooksEx** program, depending on the data entered.

    Write your design in the following space. Your design should be a list describing what happens at each line in the program, or should use the format your instructor requires.

1. b.   Write a Java program based on the design you created in Exercise 1a. Name your output file **patients.txt**. Save the program as **VBooks2.java** in the Chap12 folder on your Student Disk. Compile, execute, and test the program. Copy the instructions, input, and output that are displayed, and paste them in a block comment at the end of your program. Then print your program to submit with your work.

LAB 12.3 USING EXCEPTION HANDLING TECHNIQUES

A `catch` block either handles an exception, or it partially processes the exception, and then rethrows the same exception or another exception for the calling environment to handle the exception.

You might have multiple `try` and `catch` (or `finally`) blocks in a program. Multiple methods could each have `try` and `catch` blocks. Java keeps track of the sequence of method calls. The public method printStackTrace can be used during program development to determine the order in which the methods were called and where the exception was handled.

When an exception occurs the program can terminate, include code to recover from the exception, or log the error and continue.

Objectives

In this lab, you identify common exceptions NumberFormatException, IOException, and FileNotFoundException caused by user error and allow the user to continue.

After completing this lab, you will be able to:

- Write multiple `try` and `catch` blocks in multiple methods.
- Catch FileNotFoundException and allow the user to re-enter the filename and continue.
- Catch NumberFormatException and allow the user to re-enter the data and continue.

Estimated completion time: **120–150 minutes**

Using Exception Handling Techniques

In the following exercises, you design and write a program that uses exception handling techniques.

1. a. *Critical Thinking Exercise:* Two common errors users make when running a program are entering the incorrect data type or forgetting to insert a floppy or Zip disk for the output file. Design a program that surveys a customer for the customer's age, state, and zip code. The state should be a two-character abbreviation. Compare the two-character abbreviation for the state against a file named **states.txt** that is included in the Chap12 folder on your Student Disk. Display the user's age, state name, and zip code. Use a `finally` clause to display a message that thanks the user for participating in the survey.

   Because you may be accessing variables both within and outside the `try` block, you must declare these variables before entering the `try` block. *Hint:* To declare the input file, use BufferedReader inFile=null;

   Test your program three times by entering the data shown in Table 12-1:

Table 12-1   Testing Data

Data entry item	First test	Second test	Third test
Age	No value	Character value	Integer value
Filename	Invalid filename	"quit"	Valid filename
State	Invalid two-character state abbreviation	Valid two-character state abbreviation	Valid two-character state abbreviation
Zip code	Zip code out of the valid range	Zip code within the valid range	Zip code within the valid range

Following is a copy of the screen results that should appear after testing your program depending on the data entered.

When the user enters no value for age:

```
Please enter your age or 'q' to quit:


Thank you for participating in our survey.
```

When the user enters a character value for age:

```
Please enter your age or 'q' to quit: q


Thank you for participating in our survey.
```

When the user enters a valid value for age, an invalid filename, and "quit":

```
Please enter your age or 'q' to quit: 20
Please enter the name of your file or enter quit: nofile
Unable to open file, please insert disk, enter quit, or re-enter
the file name.

Please enter the name of your file or enter quit: quit
Thank you for participating in our survey.
```

Run your program with the following data:

- Valid value for age

- Valid filename, "states.txt"

- Invalid state two-character abbreviation, followed by a valid state two-character abbreviation

- Invalid zip code, followed by a valid zip code

When you run the program with the preceding data, the following output should be displayed:

```
Please enter your age or 'q' to quit: 20
Please enter the name of your file or enter quit: states.txt
Please enter the 2 letter state abbreviation: WS
Your state abbreviation is not valid.
Please enter the 2 letter state abbreviation or quit: TX
Please enter your zip code: 123456
Please enter your zip code: 78734

Your age: 20
Your state and zip: Texas 78734
Thank you for participating in our survey.
```

Write your design in the following space. Your design should be a list describing what happens at each line in the program, or should use the format your instructor requires.

1. b.   Write a Java program based on the design you created in Exercise 1a. For readability, insert
         blank lines to separate parts of the program. Include comments to explain the different sections
         of code. Save the program as **Address.java** in the Chap12 folder on your Student Disk.
         Compile, run, and test the program with input that tests all cases. Copy the instructions, input,
         and output that are displayed, and paste them in a block comment at the end of your program.

LAB 12.4 CREATING YOUR OWN EXCEPTION CLASSES

Java provides a substantial number of exception classes, but does not provide all the exception classes that you will ever need. Java's mechanism to process the exceptions you define is the same as that for built-in exceptions. However, you must throw your own exceptions using the throw statement.

The exception class that you define extends either the class Exception or one of its subclasses. If you have created an exception class, you can define other exception classes extending the definition of the exception class you created.

Objectives

In this lab, you create your own exception class, import the class into your program, and throw and catch the exception.

After completing this lab, you will be able to:

- Create your own exception class extending the class Exception.

- Throw an exception to the exception you create.

Estimated completion time: **60–90 minutes**

Creating Your Own Exception Classes

In the following exercises, you revise a program that includes exception classes that you create.

1. a. In Chapter 9, you wrote a program called Trucks that compares a truck's weight to an established maximum weight limit and displays a message to tell the user if the truck is within weight limits. Redesign the Trucks program to throw a checked exception when a truck's weight exceeds the limit. Write your own exception to display a dialog box that notifies the user when the weight limit is exceeded. Add a `catch` block to catch NumberFormatException exceptions. If you did not add methods to the main method, use a loop in the main method to call another method so that your program can continue after your exceptions are caught.

   Depending on the data entered, your screen results should be identical to the screen results for your Trucks program in Chapter 9, except for the additional message for invalid data. Figure 12-1 shows the screen result that should appear when no data or nonnumeric data is entered.

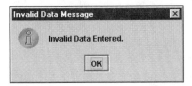

Figure 12-1 Invalid Data Message

Write your design in the following space. Your design should be a list describing what happens at each line in the program, or should use the format your instructor requires.

1. b.   Write a Java program based on the design you created in Exercise 1a. Save the program as **Trucks2.java** in the Chap12 folder on your Student Disk. Compile, execute, and test the program. Either copy the dialog boxes that appear and paste them into a document or print the screens of the dialog boxes. Then print your program to submit with your work.

LAB 12.5 USING EVENT HANDLING

An event is a specific action that triggers predefined code. Java provides various interfaces to handle different events. For example, when an action event occurs, the method actionPerformed of the interface ActionListener is executed. To create an object to handle an event, first you create a class that implements an appropriate interface.

One way to handle events in a program is to use anonymous classes. To register an action listener object to a GUI component, you use the method addActionListener. To register a window listener object to a GUI component, you use the method addWindowListener. The WindowListener object being registered is passed as a parameter to the method addWindowListener.

The following example creates an object of the anonymous class, which extends the class Window-Adapter and overrides the method windowClosing. The object created is passed as an argument to the method addWindowListener. The method addWindowListener is invoked by explicitly using the reference `this`.

```
this.addWindowListener(new WindowAdapter()
        {
            public void windowClosing(WindowEvent e)
            {
             System.exit(0);
            }
        }
    );
```

Objectives

In this lab, you use buttons to generate an action event and implement the interface ActionListener.

After completing this lab, you will be able to:

- Organize a GUI application using the methods setSize and setLocation.

- Use buttons to generate an action event.

- Implement the interface ActionListener.

Estimated completion time: **60–90 minutes**

Using Event Handling

In the following exercises, you design and write program that uses event handling.

1. a. *Critical Thinking Exercise*: Design a program to calculate a monthly loan payment and the total amount to be paid over the life of a loan. Ask the user for the amount of the loan, the interest rate, and the number of months of the loan. The user should press a button to perform the calculations and another button to reset the input and output fields. Format your GUI with labels identifying each field and buttons for calculations and to reset the fields. The actual layout is up to you to design.

The formula for calculating a loan payment is:

```
payment amount = (principle*rate/12*Math.pow(rate/12+1, time)) /
                (Math.pow(rate/12+1, time)-1);
```

Figure 12-2 shows the Loan Payment dialog box at the start of the program and when the reset button is pressed:

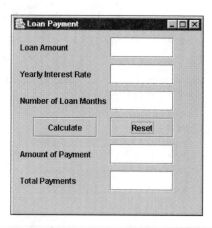

Figure 12-2   Loan Payment dialog box at the beginning of the program

Figure 12-3 shows the Loan Payment dialog box after the user has entered valid amount, interest, and month information:

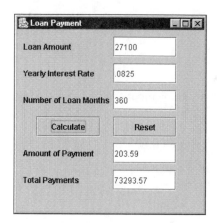

Figure 12-3   Loan Payment dialog box after user enters correct data

Figure 12-4 shows the Loan Payment dialog box after the user has entered an incorrect amount, interest, or months:

Figure 12-4   Loan Payment dialog box after user enters incorrect data

Write your design in the following space. Your design should be a list describing what happens at each line in the program, or should use the format your instructor requires.

1. b.   Write a Java program based on the design you created in Exercise 1a. Save the program as **LoanPay.java** in the Chap12 folder on your Student Disk. Compile, execute, and test the program. Either copy the dialog boxes that appear and paste them into a document or print the screens of the dialog boxes. Then print your program to submit with your work.

ADVANCED GUIS AND GRAPHICS

In this chapter, you will:

♦ Learn about applets
♦ Explore the class `Graphics`
♦ Learn about the class `Font`
♦ Explore the class `Color`
♦ Learn to use the additional Layout managers
♦ Become familiar with more GUI components
♦ Learn how to create menu-based programs
♦ Explore how to handle key and mouse events

CHAPTER 13: ASSIGNMENT COVER SHEET

Name _____   Date _____

Section _____

Lab Assignments	Grade
Lab 13.1 Creating a Java Applet Containing Formatted Strings	
Lab 13.2 Creating a Java Applet Containing Shapes (Critical Thinking Exercise)	
Lab 13.3 Converting an Application Program to an Applet	
Lab 13.4 Using additional GUI Components (Critical Thinking Exercise)	
Lab 13.5 Using Lists in Various Layouts and Using Menus	
Lab 13.6 Reviewing Key Events and Using Mouse Events	
Total Grade	

See your instructor or the introduction to this book for instructions on submitting your assignments.

LAB 13.1 CREATING A JAVA APPLET CONTAINING FORMATTED STRINGS

In Java, an applet is a Java program that is embedded in a Web page and executed by a Web browser. The class is declared public and is created by extending the class JApplet, which is contained in the package javax.swing.

A Java applet is contained in an HTML page, which includes tags that tell a browser how to interpret the HTML code. The code to be formatted is written between opening and closing tags that are not case sensitive, though it is recommended that you use uppercase letters. An opening tag is written between left and right angle brackets, as in `<TITLE>`. A closing tag is written with a left-angle bracket, a slash, the command, and a right-angle bracket, as in `</TITLE>`. Not all code requires closing tags; in fact, the browser ignores nonessential closing tags. Incorrectly written tags are also ignored.

An HTML comment begins with a left angle bracket and an exclamation mark, and ends with a dash and a right angle bracket, as in `<!--Java applet code starts here.-->`.

Use the following tags to create HTML pages for testing your Java applets:

```
<HTML>
<HEAD>
<TITLE>
            Your page name to be displayed in the title bar
</TITLE>
</HEAD>

<BODY>
            <!--Include your instruction to include your applet code.-->

<APPLET code = "NameOfApplet.class" width = "numberOfPixels" height = "
numberOfPixels ">
</BODY>
</HTML>
```

Unlike Java application programs, Java applets do not have the method main. However, you compile applets the same way that you compile any other Java program. When a browser runs an applet, the methods init, start, paint, stop, and destroy are guaranteed to be invoked in sequence. To use the various methods of the class `Graphics`, you need to import the java.awt package.

You use the init method to perform the following tasks:

- Initialize variables.

- Get data from the user.

- Place various GUI components.

The paint method has one argument, which is a Graphics object, and is used to perform output. The init and paint methods need to share common data items, so these common data items are the data members of the applet. The method drawstring displays the string specified by str at the horizontal position x pixels away from the upper-left corner of the applet, and the vertical position y pixels away from the upper-left corner of the applet.

To show text in different fonts, you use the class `Font`, contained in the package java.awt. You specify the font face name, style, and size expressed in points, where 72 points equal one inch. For example, the following code creates a 12-point italic font named Serif:

```
new Font("Serif", Font.ITALIC, 12)
```

The following code creates a 36-point italic and bold font named Dialog:

```
new Font("Dialog", Font.ITALIC + Font.BOLD, 36)
```

Java provides the class `Color` in the package java.awt to change the color of text or the background color of a component. The color scheme known as RGB, where R stands for red, G for green, and B for blue, is used to mix the amounts of red, green, and blue hues. These hues are represented in integer values 0 through 255. The value 0 means no amount of the color indicated will be used. For example, the value for white is 255, 255, 255 and the value for black is 0, 0, 0. The gray color 100,100,100 is darker than the gray color 200, 200, 200.

Objectives

In this lab, you create a Java applet and the HTML page to contain the applet.

After completing this lab exercise, you will be able to:

- Create an HTML page that calls an applet.
- Create a Java applet that displays formatted strings.
- Format strings for font face, style, size, and color.
- Use a Java applet to create a cover sheet for your programs.

Estimated completion time: **50–60 minutes**

Creating a Java Applet Containing Formatted Strings

In the following exercises, you design and write a Java applet that contains formatted text.

1. a. Design a Java applet that creates a cover sheet you can use to submit your programs to your instructor. Use the following `Font` face names, styles, sizes, and colors to identify your chapter title, name, assignment date, and class section (or any other information required by your instructor):

   - Font names: Arial, Courier, Dialog, Serif
   - Font styles: plain, italic, bold, bold italic
   - Font sizes: 18, 24, 30, 42 points
   - Font colors: red, green, blue, orange

Following is an example of one screen result that appears after running appletviewer with your HTML page depending on the font face, style, and size chosen.

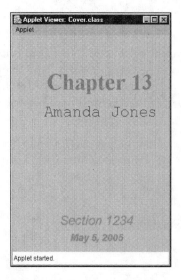

Figure 13-1   Cover applet

Write your design in the following space. Your design should be a list describing what happens at each line in the program, or should use the format your instructor requires.

1. b.   Write a Java class based on the design you created in Exercise 1a, and name it **Cover.java**. Save the program in your classes folder on your hard disk (or the location specified by your instructor).

Compile your class to be used later. (You cannot run your class code because you have not created an HTML page to activate your applet.)

1. c.   Create an HTML page that invokes the applet Cover.class. Save your page as **Cover.htm**. Run the appletviewer with your Cover.htm page or open your page in a browser. Either copy the Applet Viewer dialog box that appears and paste it into a document, or print the screen that displays the HTML page.

LAB 13.2 CREATING A JAVA APPLET CONTAINING SHAPES

The class `Graphics` also provides methods for drawing items such as lines, ovals, rectangles, and polygons on the screen. For example, you use the method drawLine to designate the location of a line by specifying the *x* and *y* coordinates from the beginning point to the *x* and *y* coordinates of the ending point. You use the method drawRect to draw a rectangle by specifying the *x* and *y* coordinates of the upper-left corner, the width *w*, and the height *h* of the rectangle.

Objectives

In this lab, you design rectangles and an oval to create flags, and fill the shapes with the colors of a flag. You determine which flag is displayed by randomly generating a number between 0 and 3 to display one of four different flags. Your completed flags should be three units wide by two units high.

After completing this lab, you will be able to:

■ Create a Java applet that displays filled rectangles and ovals.

Estimated completion time: **50–60 minutes**

Creating a Java Applet Containing Shapes

In the following exercises, you design and write a Java program that draws shapes.

1. a. *Critical Thinking Exercise*: Create a Java applet that fills rectangles and an oval to represent flags. Use a random-number generator to determine which flag is represented. Use the following values:

   ■ 0 to represent the French flag using three horizontal rectangles of the same size with the colors blue, white, and red.

   ■ 1 to represent the Austrian flag using three vertical rectangles of the same size with the colors red, white, and red.

   ■ 2 to represent the Spanish flag with three horizontal rectangles, in which the top and bottom rectangles are red and each fill 25 percent of the total rectangle. The center rectangle is yellow and fills 50 percent of the rectangle.

   ■ 3 to represent the Bangladesh flag, which is green with a red circle left of the center.

Figures 13-2 to 13-5 show examples of each flag in dialog boxes that appear after running appletviewer with your HTML page.

Figure 13-2   French flag

Figure 13-3 Austrian flag

Figure 13-4 Spanish flag

Figure 13-5 Bangladesh flag

Write your design in the following space. Your design should be a list describing what happens at each line in the program, or should use the format your instructor requires.

1. b. Write a Java class based on the design you created in Exercise 1a, and name it **Flags.java**. Save the program in your classes folder on your hard disk (or the location specified by your instructor).

Compile your class to be used later. (You cannot run your class code because you have not created an HTML page to activate your applet.)

1. c. Create an HTML page that invokes the applet Flags.class. Save your page as **Flags.htm**. Run the appletviewer with your Flags.htm page several times or open your page in a browser until all options have executed. Either copy the AppletViewer dialog boxes that appear and paste them into a document, or print the screens that display the HTML pages.

LAB 13.3 CONVERTING AN APPLICATION PROGRAM TO AN APPLET

To convert a GUI application to an applet, you must do the following:

■ Extend the definition of the class JApplet by changing JFrame to JApplet.

■ Change the constructor to the method init.

■ Remove method calls such as setVisible, setTitle, and setSize.

■ Remove the method main.

■ Remove the Exit button and all code associated with it, such as the action listener, etc.

Objectives

In this lab, you convert a GUI application to an applet.

After completing this lab, you will be able to:

■ Convert a GUI application to an applet.

Estimated completion time: **20–30 minutes**

Converting an Application Program to an Applet

In the following exercises, you revise Java programs you've already written so that they become graphical applets.

1. a.   Copy the **LoanPay** program from your Chap12 folder to your Chap13 folder. Save the program as **LoanPay2.java**. Make the changes required to convert a GUI application to an applet.

Following is an example of one screen result that appears after running appletviewer with your HTML page depending on the data entered.

Figure 13-6 shows the dialog box displayed at the start of the program and after the Reset button is clicked:

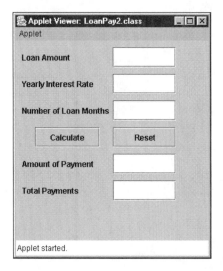

Figure 13-6   Loan payment GUI at start or reset

Figure 13-7 shows the dialog box displayed after the user has entered the amount, interest, and months:

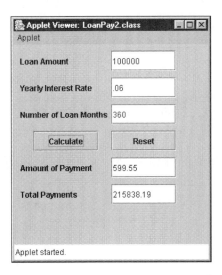

Figure 13-7   Loan payment GUI after calculation

Figure 13-8 shows the dialog box displayed after the user has entered an incorrect amount, interest, or months:

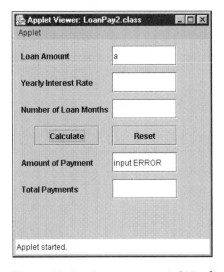

Figure 13-8   Loan payment GUI after input error

1. b. Compile your class to be used later. (You cannot run your class code because you have not created an HTML page to activate your applet.)

1. c. Create an HTML page that invokes the applet LoanPay2.class. Save your page as **LoanPay2.htm**. Run the appletviewer with your LoanPay2.htm page or open your page in a browser. Either copy the Applet Viewer dialog boxes that appear and paste them into a document, or print the screen that displays the HTML page.

LAB 13.4 USING ADDITIONAL GUI COMPONENTS

Java provides additional GUI components to display and input data. The class JTextArea allows multiple lines for input and output. Other methods used with the class JTextArea include setColumns(), setRows(), append(), setLineWrap(), setWrapStyleWord(), and setTabSize(). Inherited methods include setText(), getText(), and setEditable().

The JCheckBox and JRadioButton classes allow a user to select a value from a set of given values. Both of these classes are subclasses of the abstract class ToggleButton. To select or deselect a check box, you click the check box. When you click a JCheckBox it generates an item event. Item events are handled by the interface ItemListener that contains the abstract method itemStateChanged. You can select multiple check boxes; however, you can select only one radio button in a group. To make sure that the user can select only one radio button at a time, you create a button group and group the radio buttons.

You use a combo box, commonly known as a drop-down list, to select an item from a list of options. A JComboBox generates an ItemEvent that is monitored by an ItemListener, which invokes the method itemStateChanged exactly as in JCheckBox or JRadioButton.

Objectives

In this lab, you become acquainted with the GUI components JTextArea, JCheckBox, JRadioButton, and JComboBox.

After completing this lab, you will be able to:

- Use a JTextArea, JCheckBox, JRadioButton, and JComboBox in an applet.

Estimated completion time: **180–210 minutes**

Using Additional GUI Components

In the following exercises, you work with different GUI components. Due to the time it takes to create the GUI layout, you are not required to test the data for validity.

1. a. *Critical Thinking Exercise*: Design a Java applet that provides a form to survey computer usage. After completing the form, the user should press the Submit button. A dialog box should show the user what was input. Create a Reset button so that the user can clear the form.

   Hint: To reset the JComboBox, use the setSelectedItem() method with the first element of the list. You can choose any layout you wish. The form should include the following elements:

   - Text fields for first name, last name, street address, city, state, zip, e-mail, and computer store name.

   - A combo box with a list of computer stores and a choice of "other."

   - Check boxes to select the type of computer.

   - Radio boxes to select what is important in a computer purchase.

   - A text area for comments.

   Figures 13-9 to 13-11 show examples of the screen results that appear after running the appletviewer with your HTML page.

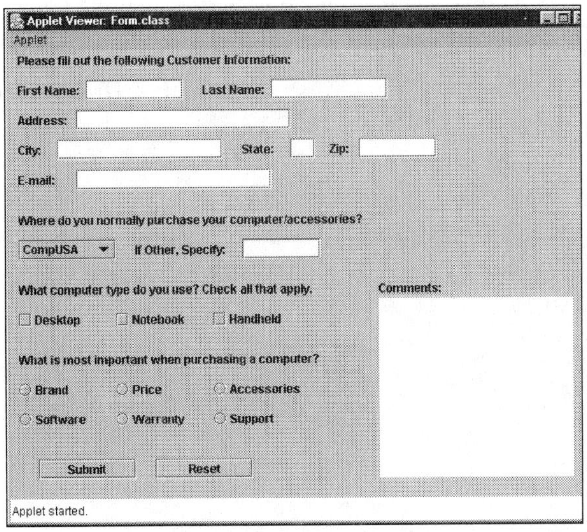

Figure 13-9   Computer survey form at start or at restart

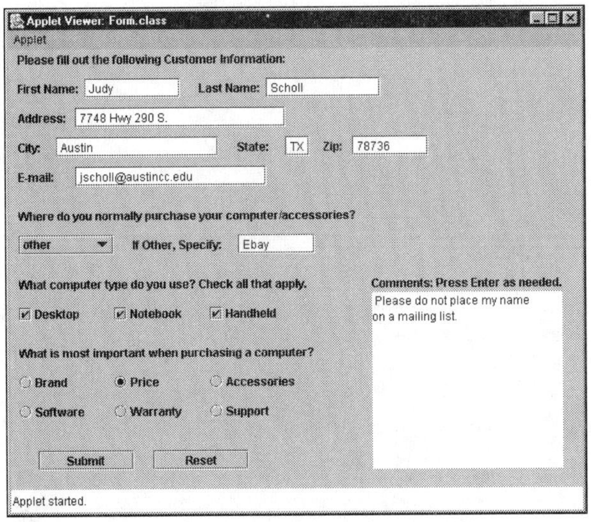

Figure 13-10   Completed computer survey form

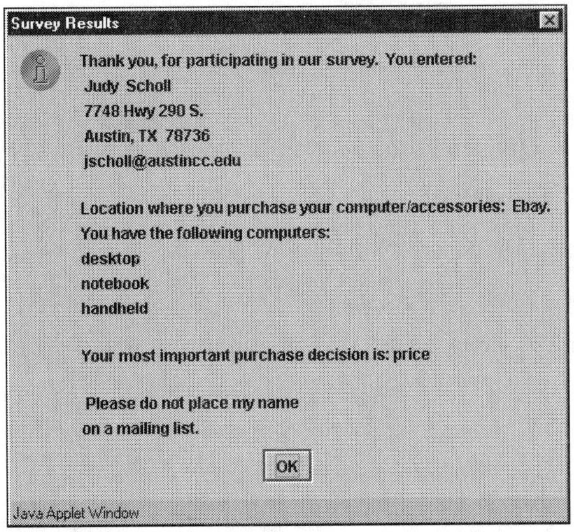

Figure 13-11   Survey Results dialog box

Write your design in the following space. Your design should be a list describing what happens at each line in the program, or should use the format your instructor requires.

1. b.   Write a Java class based on the design you created in Exercise 1a, and name it **Form.java**. Save the program in your classes folder on your hard disk (or the location specified by your instructor).

Compile your class to be used later. (You cannot run your class code because you have not created an HTML page to activate your applet.)

1. c.   Create an HTML page that invokes the applet Form.class. Save your page as **Form.htm**. Run the appletviewer with your Form.htm page or open your page in a browser. Either copy the Applet Viewer dialog boxes that appear and paste them into a document, or print the screens that display the HTML page.

Lab 13.5 Using Lists in Various Layouts and Using Menus

A list displays a number of items from which the user can select one or more. Creating a JList is similar to creating a JComboBox. Like JComboBox, you can also designate the number of rows shown in a list and restrict the list to single selection.

You can select an item on the list and display an image corresponding to the item selected. To process ListSelectionEvent, you use the interface ListSelectionListener. The interface has the method valueChanged. You can determine the index of the selected item by using the method getSelectedIndex. You use this index to select the corresponding image from the pictures array and the name of the image from the pictureNames array. Then you use the method repaint to repaint the pane.

Java provides many layout managers. You have already used GridLayout and null. Another layout is the default layout manager called FlowLayout. In GridLayout, all rows have the same number of components and all components have the same size. In FlowLayout, you can align each line either left, center, or right using a statement such as the following:

```
flowLayoutMgr.setAlignment(FlowLayout.RIGHT);
```

The default alignment is left.

The BorderLayout manager allows you to place items in specific regions. This manager divides the container into five regions: NORTH, SOUTH, EAST, WEST, and CENTER. NORTH and SOUTH span horizontally from one edge of the container to the other. EAST and WEST components extend vertically between the components in the NORTH and SOUTH regions. The component placed at the CENTER expands to occupy any unused regions. See Figure 13-12.

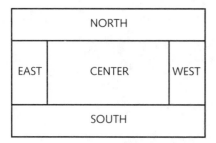

Figure 13-12   Five regions in the BorderLayout manager

Menus allow you to provide various functions without cluttering the GUI with too many components. The classes JFrame and JApplet both have a method setJMenuBar that allows you to set a menu bar. The order in which you add menus to the menu bar determines the order in which they appear.

Objectives

In this lab, you become acquainted with using lists in various layouts and with using a menu bar instead of a list.

After completing this lab, you will be able to:

- Write a program with a list using the null layout.
- Rewrite a program with a list using FlowLayout.
- Rewrite a program with a list using BorderLayout.
- Rewrite a program using a menu bar.

Estimated completion time: **120–150 minutes**

Using Lists in Various Layouts and Using Menus

In the following exercises, you work with different layouts.

1. a. Design a Java program that uses a list with the names of four different flags. Display the flag that corresponds with each list item when the item is clicked. Use the null layout and the four flag GIF files stored in the Chap13 folder of your Student Disk named **Italy.gif**, **Japan.gif**, **JollyRoger.gif**, and **US.gif**.

Figures 13-13 to 13-16 show the screen results that might appear after running your program depending on the sizes and locations that you choose.

Figure 13-13   Flag Viewer showing the U.S. flag

Figure 13-14   Flag Viewer showing the Italian flag

Figure 13-15   Flag Viewer showing the Jolly Roger flag

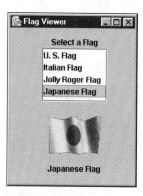

Figure 13-16   Flag Viewer showing the Japanese flag

Write your design in the following space. Your design should be a list describing what happens at each line in the program, or should use the format your instructor requires.

1. b. Write a Java program based on the design you created in Exercise 1a. Save the program as **Flags2.java** in the Chap13 folder on your Student Disk. Compile, execute, and test the program by clicking each item in the list. Either copy the windows that appear and paste them into a document, or print the screens of the windows. Then print your program to submit with your work.

2. Rewrite the program you created in Exercise 1 to use FlowLayout. Save the program as **Flags3.java** in the Chap13 folder on your Student Disk. Compile, execute, and test the program by clicking each item in the list. Either copy the windows that appear and paste them into a document, or print the screens of the windows. Then print your program to submit with your work.

Figure 13-17 shows an example of one screen result that might appear after running your program.

Figure 13-17   Flag Viewer using FlowLayout

3. Rewrite the program you created in Exercise 1 to use BorderLayout. Save the program as **Flags4.java** in the Chap13 folder on your Student Disk. Compile, execute, and test the program by clicking each item in the list. Either copy the windows that appear and paste them into a document, or print the screens of the windows. Then print your program to submit with your work.

Figure 13-18 shows an example of one screen result that might appear after running your program.

Figure 13-18   Flag Viewer using BorderLayout

4. Rewrite the program you created in Exercise 1 to use a menu. Save the program as **Flags5.java** in the Chap13 folder on your Student Disk. Compile, execute, and test the program by clicking each item in the list. Either copy the windows that appear and paste them into a document, or print the screens of the windows. Then print your program to submit with your work.

Figure 13-19 shows an example of one screen result that might appear after running your program.

Figure 13-19   Flag Viewer using a menu

LAB 13.6 REVIEWING KEY EVENTS AND USING MOUSE EVENTS

In Chapter 12 you learned that when you press a key in a text field, an action event is generated. When you press a mouse button to click a button on a form, in addition to generating an action event, a mouse event is generated. Likewise, when you press the Enter key in a text field, in addition to the action event, a key event is generated. Therefore, a GUI program can simultaneously generate more than one event.

There are three types of key events. The interface KeyListener contains the methods-keyPressed, keyReleased, and keyTyped—that correspond to these events. When you press a meta key (such as Control, Shift, or Alt), the method keyPressed is executed; when you type a regular alphanumeric key, the method keyTyped is executed. When you release any key, the method keyReleased is executed.

A mouse can generate seven different types of events. The events mouseClicked, mouseEntered, mouseExited, mousePressed, and mouseReleased are handled by MouseListener. The events mouseDragged and mouseMoved are handled by the interface MouseMotionListener.

Objectives

In this lab, you become acquainted with using mouse events.

After completing this lab, you will be able to:

- Display an image when the mouseEntered event occurs.

- Display text when the mouseExited event occurs.

Estimated completion time: **50–60 minutes**

Reviewing Key Events and Using Mouse Events

In the following exercises, you design and write a program that displays an image in response to a mouse event.

1. a. Design a program that displays a label "Fat Cat." When a mouseEntered event occurs on the label, show the image **fatcat1.gif**, which is stored in the Chap13 folder on your Student Disk. When the mouseExited event occurs, show the text "Fat Cat."

Figures 13-20 and 13-21 show examples of screen results that appear after running your program depending on the layout that you choose. (Fat Cat image is courtesy of Don Gosselin.)

Figure 13-20   Fat Cat text

Figure 13-21   Fat Cat image

Write your design in the following space. Your design should be a list describing what happens at each line in the program, or should use the format your instructor requires.

1. b. Write a Java class based on the design you created in Exercise 1a, and name it **catPic.java**. Compile, execute, and test the program by using the mouse to point to the text and then moving the mouse away from the image. Either copy the windows that appear and paste them into a document, or print the screens of the windows. Then print your program to submit with your work.

CHAPTER

14

RECURSION

In this chapter, you will:

♦ Learn about recursive definitions

♦ Explore the base case and the general case of a recursive definition

♦ Learn about recursive algorithms

♦ Learn about recursive methods

♦ Become aware of direct and indirect recursion

♦ Explore how to use recursive methods to implement recursive algorithms

297

CHAPTER 14: ASSIGNMENT COVER SHEET

Name _____   Date _____

Section _____

Lab Assignments	Grade
Lab 14.1 Designing and Implementing a void Recursive Method	
Lab 14.2 Designing and Implementing a Value-Returning Recursive Method (Critical Thinking Exercise)	
Lab 14.3 Using Recursive Methods instead of Looping	
Lab 14.4 Using a Recursive Method as Part of an Expression (Critical Thinking Exercise)	
Total Grade	

See your instructor or the introduction to this book for instructions on submitting your assignments.

LAB 14.1 DESIGNING AND IMPLEMENTING A VOID RECURSIVE METHOD

One way to repeat code is through looping structures. Another method is called recursion. A recursive method is one that calls itself. A recursive definition is one in which something is defined as a smaller version of itself. Recursion, like a loop, stops when a certain condition is met. The condition that causes the recursive method to stop is called the base case of the recursive method.

In recursion a set of statements is repeated by having the method call itself. Moreover, a selection control structure is used to control the repeated calls in recursion.

- Every recursive definition must have one or more base cases.
- The general case must eventually be reduced to a base case.
- The base case stops the recursion.

A recursive method in which the last statement executed is the recursive call is called a tail recursive method.

Objectives

In this lab, you design and implement a Java program that calls a void recursive method to reverse the elements of a string.

After completing this lab, you will be able to:

- Design and implement an algorithm to use a void recursive method.
- Use a recursive method for string processing.

Estimated completion time: **50–60 minutes**

Designing and Implementing a void Recursive Method

Suppose you want to reverse a string value. For instance, a string with a value of "Hello" would be displayed as "olleH". To help design the algorithm, first answer a few questions. Because all program designs need to consider input, processing, and output, start by determining how you want to accomplish these tasks.

1. How will the program declare your reference variable?

2. How will the value of the reference variable be input—as an assigned value or entered by the user?

3. Do you need to know the exact length or only the maximum length of the reference variable?

4. What information (arguments) should the driver program pass to the recursive method?

5. How do you know when the recursive method has reached the base case?

6. Will you display the reversed reference variable element by element or as another reference variable?

7. If you send the reference variable and the length of the string to the recursive method, you always know the last element of the reference variable. What would you do to process the reference variable by a different last character each time?

8. Write your program design in the space provided. Your design should be a list describing what happens at each line in the program, or should use the format your instructor requires.

9. a. Design a program that calls a method to display a string in reverse order. Display your original string and then your string in reverse order.

Following is a copy of the screen results that might appear after running your program, depending on the data entered. The user's input appears in bold.

Instructions:

```
This program asks a user to enter a message.
The message is then displayed in reverse order.
```

Input:

```
Please enter a message: Hello
```

Output:

```
Your message in reverse is: olleH
```

9. b. Save the program as **Reverse.java** in the Chap14 folder on your Student Disk. After executing your program, select and copy everything that appears on your screen. Paste the copied text into a comment block at the end of your program.

Lab 14.2 Designing and Implementing a Value-Returning Recursive Algorithm

If every recursive call results in another recursive call, the recursive method (algorithm) is said to have infinite recursion. Every call to a recursive method requires the system to allocate memory for the local variables, formal parameters, and information that allows control to be transferred back to the right caller. Infinite recursion will cause the system to run out of memory and abnormally terminate. Design your algorithm to meet the following criteria:

- Understand the problem requirements.

- Determine the limiting conditions.

- Identify the base cases and provide a direct solution to each base case.

- Identify the general case and provide a solution to each general case in terms of a smaller version of itself.

Objectives

In this lab, you design and write a Java program that uses a void recursive method call instead of a looping structure.

After completing this lab, you will be able to:

- Design and implement an algorithm that uses a recursive call as part of a value-returning expression to a recursive call.

Estimated completion time: **50–60 minutes**

Designing and Implementing a Value-Returning Recursive Algorithm

Critical Thinking Exercise: Design an algorithm to find the value of n raised to the power of x or (n^x). Design a program to use this algorithm as a recursive method. Your method should have arguments for base, exponent, and answer and return the integer value answer. The base and exponent value must be greater than or equal to zero. To help design the algorithm, first answer the questions in the following exercises.

Use the `try` block to parse the integer input. Use the `catch` block to end the recursion using the NumberFormatException exception, and use the `finally` block to return the number from the recursive method.

Because all program designs need to consider input, processing, and output, answer the following questions to determine how you want to accomplish these tasks.

1. How will the values for your base and exponent be input—by assignment or by interactive input?

2. The program driver might restrict valid input. However, your method should accommodate all integer values. How will you accommodate negative exponents?

3. How will you accommodate zero exponents?

4. How will you accumulate the values returned from the recursive method?

5. How will you display the result from the method calls?

6. a.   Design the program from the problem description. Your design should be a list describing what happens at each line in the program, or should use the format your instructor requires.

Following is a copy of the screen results that might appear after running your program, depending on the data entered. The user's input appears in bold.

Instructions:

```
This program asks a user to enter a base number and an exponent.
The answer is calculated and displayed.
```

Input and output:

```
Please enter your base number and your exponent (q to quit): 0 0
The number 0 raised to the power of 0 is 1.

Please enter your base number and your exponent (q to quit): 0 4
The number 0 raised to the power of 4 is 0.

Please enter your base number and your exponent (q to quit): 4 4
The number 4 raised to the power of 4 is 256.

Please enter your base number and your exponent (q to quit): 4 2
The number 4 raised to the power of 2 is 16.

Please enter your base number and your exponent (q to quit): q
Thank you for using the Power program.
```

6. b.   Save the program as **Power.java** in the Chap14 folder on your Student Disk. After executing your program, select and copy everything that appears on your screen. Paste the copied text into a comment block at the end of your program.

LAB 14.3 USING RECURSIVE METHODS INSTEAD OF LOOPING

When designing a recursive method, consider that a recursive method executes more slowly than its iterative counterpart. On slower computers, especially those with limited memory space, the slow execution of a recursive method would be visible. On newer computers with a large amount of memory space, the execution of a recursive method is not noticeable.

A program design for a recursive method is very similar to a program design for a loop.

Objectives

In this lab, you redesign and implement a Java program that you previously wrote using loops.

After completing this lab, you will be able to:

- Design programs using recursive methods instead of loops.

Estimated completion time: **50–60 minutes**

Using Recursive Methods Instead of Looping

In the following exercises, you redesign and revise a program to use recursive methods instead of looping.

1. a.   In Lab 5.1, Exercise 3, you designed a repetition program named **Find1.java** to search an input file for a particular item. Refer to that design to redesign the program to use a recursive method. Your design should be a list describing what happens at each line in the program, or should use the format your instructor requires.

1. b. Copy the file **invoice1.dat** from your Chap05 folder into your Chap14 folder. Write a Java program based on the design you created in Exercise 1a. Save the program as **FRecur.java** in the Chap14 folder on your Student Disk, and then compile, run, and test the program. Either copy the dialog boxes that appear and paste them into a document, or print screens of the dialog boxes. Depending on the data entered, your output should be identical to the output of your **Find1.java** program in Chapter 5.

Test your program with the file **invoice1.dat** and with the following input:

```
shovel
```

Print your input file and program and attach them to your printed output screens to submit with your work.

LAB 14.4 USING A RECURSIVE METHOD AS PART OF AN EXPRESSION

When a statement calls a recursive method as part of an expression, it is a recursive call. Processing a value that returns a recursive method is called unwinding the recursion.

Objectives

In this lab, you design and implement a Java program that uses a recursive call as part of an expression.

After completing this lab, you will be able to:

- Use Java to implement the design of an algorithm that uses a recursive call as part of an expression.

- Use the returned value from a recursive call to add to a value that is an accumulator.

Estimated completion time: **50–60 minutes**

Using a Recursive Method as Part of an Expression

In the following exercises, you design and write a program that uses a recursive method to reverse the order of integers.

1. a. *Critical Thinking Exercise*: Design a program that uses a recursive method to reverse the order of integers. For example, if you have an integer with a value 5982, the displayed integer should be 2895. Do not convert the integer as a string. You must calculate it as an integer. Display the starting number and the ending number.

    Following is a copy of the screen results that might appear after running your program, depending on the data entered. The user's input appears in bold.

    Instructions:

    ```
    This program asks a user to enter a number.
    The number is then displayed in reverse order.
    ```

    Input and output:

    ```
    This program asks a user to enter a number.
    The number is then displayed in reverse order.

    Please enter a positive number (q to quit): 123456
    Your number 123456 written in reverse is 654321.

    Please enter a positive number (q to quit): 456543
    Your number 456543 written in reverse is 345654.

    Please enter a positive number (q to quit): 9807
    Your number 9807 written in reverse is 7089.

    Please enter a positive number (q to quit): 1
    Your number 1 written in reverse is 1.

    Please enter a positive number (q to quit): q
    Thank you for using the reverse number program.
    ```

    Write your design in the following space. Your design should be a list describing what happens at each line in the program, or should use the format your instructor requires.

1. b.   Write a Java program based on the design you created in Exercise 1a. Save the program as **IntRev.java** in the Chap14 folder on your Student Disk. Compile, run, and test the program with the input shown in Exercise 1a. Copy the instructions, input, and output that are displayed, and then paste them in a block comment at the end of your program.

Index